D0078327

THEORY OF SUSPENSIONS

Number Five in the Princeton Studies in Music

THEORY OF SUSPENSIONS

*A Study of Metrical and Pitch Relations
in Tonal Music*

By Arthur J. Komar

PRINCETON UNIVERSITY PRESS, PRINCETON, N.J. 1971

FOREWORD

For the first chapter of a book to contain a general introduction is nothing other than appropriate; but precedent is violated in the present case, inasmuch as two additional chapters stand between the introductory chapter and the chapters dealing with suspensions per se. The first of these additional chapters involves a discussion of the terminology of tonal theory; and I trust that this attempt at preventive clarification requires no further justification. The second additional chapter presents a theory of meter—the need for which is a somewhat more complex matter.

Suspension configurations involve both metrical and pitch relations. I am under no obligation to formulate a theory of pitch relations, since the basis for a satisfactory formulation already exists in the writings of Heinrich Schenker—particularly in his final work, *Der freie Satz*.[1] Assuming the reader's familiarity with Schenker's basic ideas, I can proceed to discuss the pitch aspect of suspension configurations with no further reference to pitch relations than necessarily arises in the chapter on terminology (Chapter Two). There is, however, no comparable theory of meter to fall back upon, and yet the metrical aspect of suspension configurations is no less prominent than the pitch aspect. In the absence of a theory of meter, the general tendency is simply to accept the notated metrical relations in a piece as given; but, of course, metrical notations are merely symptomatic, rather than determinant, of metrical structure. Even more important is the fact that large-scale metrical relations are not even included in conventional notation. And where metrical relations are notated, it is not unusual to find ambiguous or misleading passages—as in the case of an essentially duple structure which is notated in triple meter. Inappropriate notation of this kind has no effect on the basic metrical structure of the passage; the question always remains whether a given beat

---

1 Volume III of *Neue Musikalische Phantasien und Theorien,* Vienna, 1935; revised edition, 1956.

sounds like a strong or weak beat, with respect to other beats, regardless of notated appearances. Unless and until criteria for determining genuine metrical relations are established, little can meaningfully be said about the metrical characteristics of suspension configurations.

In view of these considerations, the reader should not be surprised to find a substantial portion of the book devoted to introductory matters, before attention is focused on the suspension, as implied by the title.

This book originated in substantially its present form as a doctoral dissertation accepted by the Department of Music of Princeton University. The readers were Godfrey Winham and Milton Babbitt.

During the last several years, I have discussed various problems in the theory of tonal music with Godfrey Winham, to whom I am indebted both for the formulation of some basic ideas about rhythm, as well as for critical judgments about the general contents of this book. We have had so many conversations about rhythm in tonal music that I cannot faithfully account for which ideas were his before becoming enmeshed in my own thinking. Therefore, he should not be held responsible for any single part of this book, but should take credit for any value in the work as a whole.

The importance of Milton Babbitt in the field of tonal theory is no less pronounced than in the fields of twelve-tone and electronic music theory, for which he is most well known. So although in writing this book I worked with Professor Babbitt less directly than with Dr. Winham, I trust that Professor Babbitt's influence will not go unappreciated. I wish to express my appreciation also to Kenneth Levy, Chairman of the Princeton Music Department; and to the members of the Publications Committee of the Princeton Music Department, Milton Babbitt, Edward T. Cone, and Lewis Lockwood.

I have made numerous revisions with the goal of clarifying individual points and making the book generally more accessible to the reader. I have been ably assisted in this effort by three colleagues who offered critical suggestions: David Epstein (Massachusetts Institute of Technology), John Rogers (University of New Hampshire), and George Todd (Middlebury College).

Finally, I wish to thank those most directly involved in converting the manuscript into a book. Lalor Cadley, Managing Editor of Princeton University Press, supervised production, with the assistance of Linda Peterson. The manuscript was copyedited by Eve Hanle and set by Caroline Browne. John Davis, of Music-Book Associates, autographed the music samples.

Newton Highlands, Massachusetts
August 1969

CONTENTS

THEORY OF SUSPENSIONS

CHAPTER ONE

INTRODUCTION†

In the literature of tonal theory, the suspension has not received attention commensurate with its compositional significance and widespread use. Numerous questions remain unanswered—indeed, unasked—such as: Why is a suspension resolved only by step? In what sense is a resolution delayed? To what end the proverbial dissonance of suspensions, and how is it that some suspensions are nonetheless consonant? In fact, precisely how does one determine whether a suspension is consonant or dissonant? Why is a suspension ordinarily metrically accented with respect to its resolution, and, more generally, just what *is* metrical accent? And, perhaps most important of all, why is the suspension so prominent in tonal music?

The dearth of answers to these questions follows in large measure from the absence of a satisfactory theory of tonal rhythm. A theory of rhythm is indispensable for describing suspensions, because even in its melodic and harmonic aspects the suspension is fundamentally a rhythmic phenomenon.

The melodic aspect of suspension configurations, i.e., the stepwise relation between suspension and resolution, follows from the different rhythmic implications of an arpeggiated skip versus those of a linear succession. For although the first note of an arpeggiated skip is not normally thought of as delaying the second note, the first note of a linear succession might well be regarded as holding back the attack of its successor. (See "Linear Relationships" and "Suspension Configuration," Chapter Two, Sections 6 and 7, pp. 38-47, below.)

Similarly, the characteristic harmonic relationships associated with suspension configurations are dependent upon the idea that notes which provide chordal support for a given note

---

† Numerous technical terms employed in this chapter are defined elsewhere in this study, mainly in Chapter Two. See also the Index of Definitions and Explications, pp. 165-166, below.

may remain in the original time-span of that note, even when its own attack is subsequently delayed. It follows from this idea that the attack of a suspension in lieu of its resolution results in the proverbial dissonance of suspensions, due to the harmonic conjunction of the suspension with the notes originally supporting the resolution. (See pp. 45-46 and "The dissonant suspension," pp. 81ff., below.) Assertions of this sort are within the domain of rhythmic theory as well as the domain of harmonic theory, since they involve the relocation of the attack-points of harmonically associated notes.

The need for a foundational rhythmic theory is most acute with regard to the purely rhythmic aspect of suspension configurations. The suspension operation alters the location and duration of notes generated in given time-spans at prior levels. If this operation were merely an optional, indirect way of placing notes in a (second) set of time-spans, i.e., if one could place the notes in these time-spans to begin with, then there would be little interest in this operation. It is only because the results of the suspension operation tend *not* to duplicate results of other operations that the suspension is of such importance in tonal composition. (For further discussion of this point, see pp. 27 and 44, below.) To put it another way, some types of rhythmic configurations can be generated in one way, while others are derivable only from those configurations generated in the first way. A theory of suspensions presupposes a conception of original or basic rhythmic configurations from which suspension configurations significantly differ. But this necessarily involves the use of some sort of precise rhythmic values at *all* structural levels at which suspensions are introduced, in order to specify accurately the rhythmic relationships both before and after the application of the suspension operation.

Schenker accounted for the element of pitch by formulating a system in which pitches are derived by means of a limited number of tonal operations applied successively through a series of progressively more elaborate structural levels, the first of which consists of a tonic triad, the last being the actual music. What is needed for the element of rhythm is a corresponding formulation for generating rhythmic values—or at least for providing some basis for deriving ultimate rhythmic values—from background note configurations.

A move in this direction was made recently by Ann Alexandra Pierce in "The Analysis of Rhythm in Tonal Music."[1] Mrs. Pierce correlates pitch and rhythm by locating the foreground time-points of notes originating at various structural levels. These time-points mark off time-spans of undoubted analytic significance, but Mrs. Pierce identifies them without explaining their origin. And explanations are needed; for there is every reason to suppose that background rhythmic values resemble background pitch configurations in undergoing alteration as the foreground is approached. Mrs. Pierce does not address herself to what I see as the central problem in tonal rhythm—providing a theory for deriving rhythmic values for *all* structural levels of a piece.

Attempts to account for large-scale rhythmic relationships have, of course, been made from a non-Schenkerian orientation, notably in the writings of Alfred Lorenz[2] and more recently, from a similar standpoint, in *The Rhythmic Structure of Music* by Grosvenor W. Cooper and Leonard B. Meyer,[3] and in *Musical Form and Musical Performance* by Edward T. Cone.[4] The general view to which all of these writers subscribe is that in music the accentual relationships among beats, bars, phrases, sections, *et al.* resemble the various syllabic accents of poetic feet. For example, the rhythmic relationships of the traditional musical setting of "Frère Jacques" would be manifested as a series of trochees, corresponding to the scansion of the verse. Now, in evaluating *frère* as a trochee, one makes no distinction between 1) the moment one articulates the first syllable and 2) the time which elapses between that moment and the moment

---

[1] Unpublished dissertation, Brandeis University, 1968 (available from University Microfilms, Order No. 69-5449).
[2] *Das Geheimnis der Form bei Richard Wagner*, Vols. 1-4, Berlin, 1924-1933.
[3] Chicago, 1960
[4] New York, 1968

one articulates the second syllable. One simply says that the first syllable is strong and the second one weak. On the other hand, one does make a distinction of this sort in describing the rhythmic relations in the musical setting of that word. Thus, in 4/4 meter, with *frè* on the first beat and *re* on the second beat, one says that *frè* occurs on a stronger beat than *re*; but one does not mean thereby that all the moments *between* those beats are stronger than the second beat. Quite to the contrary, all of those between-beat moments are ordinarily understood to be *weaker* than the second beat. So while it is proper to say that *frè* occurs on a stronger beat than *re*, it does not follow that the entire time-span of *frè* is stronger than the time-span of *re*. Nor do I find it meaningful to view the three sections of a sonata-form movement as a large-scale anapestic foot; cf. for example, level #5 of the Cooper and Meyer analysis of the first movement of Beethoven's Eighth Symphony.[5] Indeed, it strikes me as unprofitable to make any assertions about the relative strength of adjacent *time-spans,* as opposed to adjacent *time-points* (beats).

Aside from the treatises referred to above, one finds little else of recent origin on the subject of tonal rhythm. In his well-known harmony text,[6] Walter Piston uses the term "harmonic rhythm" to refer to the rate of chord change in a given context; but aside from pointing out that this is a significant element in tonal music and providing numerous examples, he does not indicate in a systematic way how harmonic rhythm is related to other aspects of structure. A recent article by Ingmar Bengtsson with the promising title, "On Relationships between Tonal and Rhythmic Structures in Western Multipart Music,"[7] turns out to be disappointing, because the author's (accurately stated) purpose is "neither to set forth a system, nor even lay some cornerstones of such a system, but only to attempt to present briefly the outlines of a 'synthetic' approach to tonal

[5] In *The Rhythmic Structure of Music,* p. 203.
[6] *Harmony,* New York, 1941.
[7] Ingmar Bengtsson, *Svensk Tidskrift för Musikforskning,* Vol. 43(1961), pp. 49-76.

and rhythmic phenomena which might possibly prove worthy of further development in a more systematic direction."

It would appear that Schenker's theories offer the best starting point for the formulation of a rhythmic theory, inasmuch as they deal with background note relationships from which actual foreground orderings of pitches are derived. But Schenker's views on rhythm are unclear and contradictory. On the one hand, durational values are introduced, generally without comment, only at relatively foreground levels, while durational notation is otherwise used to indicate differences in the structural weight of notes at prior levels. (See, for example, his analysis of Schumann's "Aus meinen Tränen spriessen" in *Der freie Satz*.[8]) Schenker states that "Rhythm in the *Ursatz* is as unlikely as in a *cantus-firmus* exercise in strict composition";[9] and this view is corroborated by a description of middleground-type bass prolongations as "precisely as arhythmic, ametrical and formless as the *Ursatz*."[10] On the other hand, the chapter on meter and rhythm in *Der freie Satz*[11] contains much evidence that Schenker regarded these elements as originating at levels prior to the foreground. Thus, on page 184 he writes: " . . . without repetition a metrical pattern is unthinkable. However, that these repetitions, as in general all repetitions in the foreground, receive clarification and establishment only from the background and middleground goes without saying."[12] And he presents several sketches demonstrating the expansion of even-numbered bar groupings into larger bar groupings, using durational values in the ordinary way, even at relatively background levels. Moreover, his chapter on diminution indicates very specifically how foreground rhythmic patterns can be derived from comparatively strict middleground configurations.[13]

[8] Page 71 and *Anhang,* Fig. 22b, p. 8. (All page references to *Der freie Satz* are for the revised edition.)

[9] *Ibid.,* p. 45.

[10] *Ibid.,* p. 64.

[11] *Ibid.,* pp. 183-196.

[12] *Ibid.,* p. 184.

[13] *Ibid.,* pp. 145-165.

In any case, Schenker's theories—extended to include rhythmic values derived in conjunction with pitch values—provide a basis for a theory of suspensions. Indeed, the description of both the linear and harmonic aspects of suspension configurations in this study follows directly from theoretical formulations in *Der freie Satz*. For while Schenker deals only slightly with suspensions per se in this volume, the bulk of his efforts are directed toward describing the melodic and harmonic relationships which provide the foundation for my theory of suspensions. On the other hand, my ideas with respect to the explicitly rhythmic aspects of suspension configurations are independent, representing an extension of, rather than an inference from, Schenker's formulations. It is well known that Schenker generally introduced specific rhythmic values only in the foreground; as a consequence, he could not provide precise rhythmic specifications for suspensions at background and middleground levels. Moreover, the well-known metrical aspect of suspension configurations—whereby the suspension is regarded as metrically accented with respect to its resolution—depends upon a general theory of meter, which Schenker did not supply. Without claiming the formulation of a complete theory of tonal rhythm, I attempt to account for the principal aspects of meter in Chapter Three, Sections 1-5,[14] and for the rhythmic characteristics of note configurations both prior and subsequent to the application of the suspension operation, in Chapter Three, Section 6.

I should add here that while Schenker's theories provide the foundation for my own theories about tonal music, and about suspensions in particular, I do not mean to commit myself to any particular aspect of his formulations; nor do I pretend not to deviate from or even contradict some of his ideas—especially in view of his belief that rhythm is not a feature of the background.[15] It will be helpful if the reader is already familiar with Schenker's basic ideas, especially the concept of structural levels

[14] The structural function of meter is described specifically in Section 4.
[15] See p. 7, above.

(*Schichten*); but this is not essential, inasmuch as I include a fairly extensive exposition of those ideas in the discussion of terminology in Chapter Two. Since an English translation of Schenker's writings with an authoritative glossary of English equivalents for the original German terms is not readily available, I have used whichever English terms strike me as most suitable.

In spite of the familiar prominence of the suspension in tonal music, the question "Why is a suspension used in a particular context?" has rarely been raised in the theoretical literature. Chapter Four considers the main reasons for the compositional use of suspensions. This discussion, which is illustrated with numerous examples from the literature, includes a detailed examination of the harmonic contexts in which suspensions are found; an account of the sense in which suspensions are dissonant or consonant; and an explanation of the correlation between the harmonic context of a given suspension and its compositional use. In addition, this chapter surveys the function of the 'large-scale suspension'—a suspension introduced at a background or middleground level. Finally, Chapter Five takes up analytical problems involving suspensions, including the problem of differentiating between suspensions on the one hand, and appoggiaturas, anticipations, and common-tones on the other.

No bibliography is included inasmuch as Schenker is the only author from whom I have derived my ideas. I have consulted numerous other treatises, textbooks, and articles, but in most cases the descriptions of meter and suspensions were limited, obvious, misleading, incomplete, or inaccurate. Listing these references would be a sterile task. Bibliographic references pertinent to particular aspects of this study are included in footnotes at the appropriate places in the text (e.g., earlier in this chapter and in the introduction to Chapter Four).

The musical examples are found either immediately below an initial verbal reference, or on one of the pages immediately following that reference. References to previously cited examples are provided with page numbers. In a few cases, for the convenience of the reader, I have repeated brief examples rather than refer to an original example at many pages' distance. In general, the subheadings "a" and "b," etc. for two (or more) parts of an example mean that the "b" part is derived from the "a" part, "c" is derived from "b," etc.

CHAPTER TWO

TERMS AND DEFINITIONS

Anyone familiar with the theory of tonal music knows the particular agony of expressing himself with the terminology in current use. I have not hesitated to coin new terms where this has seemed practical, but in many cases I have settled for the usual, underdefined, ambiguous terminology. Designing a set of rigorous terms for music is a serious but unfulfilled goal of current music theory. I had the choice of doing as well as possible with the available terms, or taking up the problem of terminology as an independent effort. I have compromised by devoting this chapter to a consideration of the principal terms —with the exception of those terms pertinent to meter which are included in Chapter Three. The reader will find that this chapter represents an informal introduction to my general views on tonal music (derived in good measure from Schenker) and will also discover new terms which I have coined (e.g., 'linear-note') and old terms which I use contrary to standard usage (e.g., 'voice' and 'part'). There are also numerous familiar but unclear terms which I do not define, but I trust that they will be clarified by the contexts in which they occur.

I begin with a brief discussion of some of the principal terms associated with the tonal system in general, and with suspensions in particular. A more detailed consideration of these and other terms starts on page 15, below. An Index of Definitions and Explications is found on pp. 165-166.

Following Schenker, I conceive of a tonal piece as a hierarchy of 'structural levels' (or simply, 'levels') progressing from relatively simple higher levels through middle levels of greater complexity to still more elaborate levels at the bottom of the hierarchy. The highest level of a tonal piece consists of a root-position major or minor triad, and the lowest level consists of the actual music itself. Progress from one level to the next lower level is achieved by means of 'operations.' A 'suspension' is the product of an operation applied to an ordered pair of notes —where a 'note' is understood as either a pitch-class or a pitch —at a level at which they are scalar and temporal adjacencies. The effect of the suspension operation is to extend the 'time-span' of the first note, while delaying the attack and fore-shortening the time-span of the second note. The note occupy-ing the extended time-span of the first note is the suspension proper, which may or may not be tied to the preceding first note.

More precisely, at the level prior to the appearance of the suspension, the given pair of notes occupy adjacent, non-overlapping time-spans. The newly generated suspension occupies an initial portion of the former time-span of the second note, while the second note now occupies only the latter portion of its former time-span, commencing instead at the 'time-point' which marks the completion of the time-span of the suspension. Thus, the temporal adjacency of the given note-pair remains undisturbed; but the time-point at which the second note (*qua* 'resolution') 'displaces' the first note occurs later.

To describe a note as a suspension is necessarily to invoke the notion of *two* levels: the level at which the suspension originates, and the prior level at which the note now called the resolution is understood to be attacked at the subsequent attack-point of the suspension. The delaying effect of the sus-pension operation is clearly illustrated in Fux's *Gradus ad Parnassum*[1] —see Ex. 1. Fux's lower sketch (b) represents a "background reduction" of the upper sketch. The latter consists of a sequence of 4–3 suspensions, while the former consists exclusively of parallel thirds. (Fux's vertical arrangement of the two sketches reverses the current practice of placing a fore-ground sketch below a related background sketch.)

[1] Johann Joseph Fux, *Gradus ad Parnassum,* 1725; translated and edited by Alfred Mann under the title *The Study of Counterpoint,* New York, 1965, Figs. 63 and 64, p. 56.

Ex. 1

I should add that to describe a note as suspended is not the same as describing it as maintained. Even where two notes are explicitly tied together, at least three interpretations are possible: 1) the second note is a suspension; 2) the first note is an anticipation; or 3) the second note is a common-tone. (See Chapter Five, Section 3 for further discussion of anticipations and common-tones.)

Assuming a polyphonic context, the usual harmonic effect of the suspension operation is to rhythmically realign vertically associated notes, producing at least one new chord, the 'suspension chord,' lying between the chords previously associated with the given note-pair. There is also a corresponding rhythmic intensification in cases where the suspension is not tied, i.e., due to the extra note-attack or where the total time-span of the given first note and tied suspension is syncopated. (See Chapter Three, Section 4, B regarding the concept of syncopation.) The harmonic and rhythmic complexity of suspension configurations is one indication of the progressively more elaborate character of lower levels in the hierarchical structure of a tonal piece.

The remarkable feature of the tonal system as Schenker conceived it is that a select number of the total available set of operations are applicable at all levels of a piece. (This is not to say that these select operations are applied in exactly the same way at all levels—a matter which I discuss in some detail under "Level," below.) Thus, the same operations which provide 'linear-pairs'—pairs of notes which are scalar and temporal adjacencies in addition to fulfilling certain other conditions which I describe below under "Linear Relationships"—in actual music (i.e., at the lowest levels) also prevail at higher levels. Consequently, a pair of scalar adjacencies which are apparently *not* temporally adjacent in a foreground passage may nevertheless be regarded as a linear-pair—even in cases where the time-spans of the two notes are widely separated. In such cases, the time-spans of these notes are separated only in a literal sense; in a structural sense they retain their original proximity, even though other notes, generated at lower levels, occupy intervening portions of those time-spans.

The suspension operation can be applied to a linear-pair *at any level*. This gives rise to the notion of the 'large-scale suspension'—a suspension which is widely separated from its 'preparation' and/or 'resolution' in a given musical passage, in spite of the temporal adjacency of the given linear-pair at the higher level at which the suspension originates. In using the term 'suspension' in this study, I shall refer indiscriminately to both 'local' and 'large-scale' suspensions, inasmuch as each type of suspension is temporally adjacent to its preparation and resolution at the level at which the suspension arises.

In putting forth the concept of the large-scale suspension, I am simply following Schenker, who frequently indicated large-scale suspensions in background sketches—see his analysis of Mozart's Piano Sonata in A major K. 331, 3rd movement, bars 17-24,[2] Ex. 2, below. On the other hand, in requiring that the attack-points of the constituent elements of a suspension configuration be specified at background levels, I am obviously departing from Schenker's views on the relation between rhythmic values and structure—see p. 7, above.

In the following sections I discuss a number of terms introduced in the preceding pages of this chapter. For the con-

[2] *Der freie Satz, Anhang,* Fig. 35/2, p. 11.

Ex. 2

venience of the reader who might subsequently wish to review a given term or definition, I have made no attempt to avoid redundancy in the two parts of this chapter. For a while I considered urging the reader to skip over the following pages and to consult them only as the need arose; but I now suspect that there are enough new terms and special uses of old terms to make such a recommendation inadvisable.

1. Structural Level, Level

An organizational stage of a piece or passage of music consisting of notes[3] resulting from the application of tonal or rhythmic operations* (p. 22)[4] at prior levels, and upon which such operations may in turn be performed, effecting subsequent levels. Levels are classified as background, middleground, or foreground, depending upon their relative nearness to the absolute background—consisting of an unarpeggiated chord, usually a major or minor root-position triad—or to the absolute foreground—the actual music itself. Since levels are analytic constructs, there is no empirically determined number of levels for a given context; the number varies with the analysis.

An illustration of a hierarchy of several levels is presented in Ex. 3. The highest level consists of an unarpeggiated interval,

[3] The term 'note' is understood to mean either a pitch or a pitch-class. 'Note' and 'tone' are synonymous; but I generally refrain from the use of 'tone' except in terms like 'common-tone.'
[4] An asterisk (*) followed by a page reference in parentheses indicates a term defined elsewhere in this chapter.

Ex. 3

the third E-C. Subsequently this interval is arpeggiated and then filled in by a passing-note, D; finally, the E is suspended into the time-span of D. Each level is more elaborate than the next higher level in the hierarchy.

A peculiarity of the language associated with tonal theory is that one speaks of generating a note q by virtue of some operation at level x, but note q is not *present* until the next lower level y. In other words, the act of generation is visited upon the notes of level x, but the result of that act first appears only in level y. Thus, in Ex. 3, D is generated at the second level (b) but initially appears only at the third level (c). Similarly, the suspension E is generated at the third level (c), but initially appears only at the fourth level (d). To counter the oddity of speaking of generating a note that is not actually there (at level x), it has been suggested that the preposition "from" be substituted for "at," as in "note q, generated *from* level x." Although this locution does not sit well with me, I invite the reader to make the substitution if the relation between operations and levels thereby becomes clearer.

The concept of levels would have little theoretical value in the absence of criteria for determining the kind of configurations which might occur at various types of levels, i.e., at background levels as opposed to middleground and foreground levels, etc. Another way of putting this is to say that standards are needed for indicating what kinds of configurations are suitable as the basis for the generation of other configurations, since without such standards one analysis of a given musical passage would make as much sense as any other. This is not the place for a critique of Schenker's ideas on this subject, nor for a thorough airing of my own views on this delicate matter. I shall restrict myself here to a few considerations which I hope will make the notion of distinctions between background, middle-ground, and foreground level-types both clear and meaningful.

The root-position tonic triad, which appears at the ultimate background level, may be thought of as the ideal representation of simplicity and stability. It should be noted that none of the three members of a tonic triad is diatonically adjacent to either of the other two members, but that each member can be connected to another member through a portion of a diatonic scale. In other words, the tonic triad consists exclusively of skips which can be connected by diatonic steps. The tonal operations involve the generation of diatonic steps, including neighbor-notes between repeated instances of just one triadic member, and passing-notes between different triadic members. Inasmuch as these diatonic connectors form non-triadic intervals with the triadic members which they connect, the chords resulting from their generation in a polyphonic context would necessarily include unstable and dissonant* (p. 28) intervals, in addition to stable consonant* (p. 28) intervals (see Ex. 4).

Example 5 retains the passing D of Ex. 4, but in a consonant chord; D is now a triadic fifth instead of a "non-harmonic"

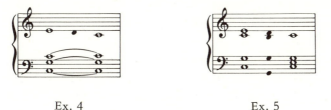

Ex. 4   Ex. 5

passing ninth. The harmonic context of Ex. 5 is once again stable and consonant—appropriate to the background—like the ultimate background level which consists of just the single tonic triad. The virtue of the all-triadic harmonic context of Ex. 5 is that each of the triads is itself a suitable basis for further 'prolongations'* (p. 23), just as all three triads together represent a prolongation of the original tonic triad at the ultimate background level. By contrast, the dissonant middle chord of Ex. 4 offers relatively little scope for possible foreground elaboration. For whereas the G major triad of Ex. 5 can be appropriately prolonged by means of the scale of G major, the dissonant middle chord of Ex. 4 has no such corresponding scale associated with it as a (secondary) tonic chord.

(Example 5 is a four-part version of Schenker's $\hat{3}$–*Ursatz* and represents what he regarded as one of the three possible background configurations [derived from a tonic triad] for a tonal piece.[5] I introduce this example here in order to illustrate consonant harmonic support for a non-tonic member of the diatonic scale, but without intending to affirm Schenker's view that the top part of a background configuration invariably descends to $\hat{1}$ from $\hat{3}$, $\hat{5}$, or $\hat{8}$. In fact, I would go even further and say that for extended pieces of music it is not always feasible to specify melodic configurations—as opposed to harmonic successions—at background levels.)

We may infer from Ex. 4 that dissonance is not suitable for background levels, insofar as the dissonant chord of that example differs so markedly from the consonant chord which characterizes the ultimate background level of any tonal piece. On the other hand, we may infer from Ex. 5 that non-tonic members of the diatonic scale are appropriate at background levels, provided that they are supported in root-position triadic harmonies.

Although block chords characterize background levels, they are also found at foreground levels, as in Ex. 6. Note, however, that the chords of Ex. 6 include inverted triads and seventh chords, as well as root-position triads, whereas only root-position chords are found at background levels. Foreground levels are also characterized by single note-attacks, but—as I have suggested with regard to Ex. 4—single note-attacks would

---

[5] *Der freie Satz*, pp. 50-53, and *Anhang*, Figs. 9-11, p. 2.

Ex. 6. Beethoven, Piano Sonata Op. 14/2, 2nd movement

generally be inappropriate at background levels. Example 7 exhibits a predominantly single-note foreground texture, while Ex. 8 offers a foreground mixture of single notes and block chords.

Ex. 7. Bach, *Well-Tempered Clavier,* Vol. 1, Prelude 5

Ex. 8. Haydn, *St. Antoni Chorale*

Middleground levels, like background levels, are characterized by root-position triads; the distinction between middleground and background levels therefore rests primarily upon non-harmonic elements. The relative size of the time-span of a prolongation corresponds directly to the level at which it arises. For example, if a particular dominant chord is to represent a background level it should be prolonged over a longer time-span than other, middleground dominants. A prominent means of achieving a large time-span is the technique of tonicization; I am referring not merely to the temporary introduction of the appropriate chromatic scale degrees, but to the actual long-term proliferation of harmonic progressions within that key-area. The slow movement of Beethoven's Piano Sonata Op. 7 offers an illustration of the distinction between middleground and background dominants (Ex. 9). The root-position V chord in

Ex. 9

bar 7 represents the main linear-chord of the first phrase, bars 1-8 (c). Another root-position V chord is prolonged as a quasi-tonic in bars 9-14 (b); local V–I progressions and new thematic material in a higher register are introduced in connection with this tonicization. In other words, the middle-ground V at bar 7 merely occurs within a section, while the more background V of bars 9-14 *represents* a section.

There is a still more background V in this movement, the attack-point of which is located at bar 37 (a). This V does not appear to represent a section in the foreground; but notice that it achieves prominence as the resolution of the large-scale prolongation of A♭ which fills much of the middle section of the movement. (The reader who is familiar with Schenker-oriented analyses might infer from Ex. 9 that I tend to locate dominants which occur progressively later in a piece at correspondingly more background levels; therefore, I hasten to add that I regard the V at bar 37 as the most background V of the movement—as I have implied in Ex. 9a. I should add that Schenker himself published sketches in which the final V of the foreground is *not* analyzed as the main background V. For example, see his analysis of the first movement of Beethoven's

Piano Sonata Op. 57,[6] as well as the schema for interruption-form [with the second V enclosed in parentheses].[7])

Another example of level differentiation between root-position dominants is found in the second movement of Beethoven's Piano Sonata Op. 13 (Ex. 10). The main V chord

Ex. 10

of the first phrase, bars 1-8, is located at bar 4. (Notice again the analysis of a non-final V [bar 4] as superior to a final V [bar 7].) I would locate the V chord of bar 23 at a more background level than the V chord of bar 4; for although E♭ is tonicized in both cases, the cadence at bar 4 is relatively unsubstantial compared to the hefty authentic cadence at bar 23. Also, D♮ (the 7th degree of the E♭ major scale) is introduced three whole bars before the cadence at bar 23, whereas D♮ occurs just an eighth-note before the cadence at bar 4. (A score and metrical analysis of this movement are found in the Appendix.)

Example 11 exhibits an *Ursatz*-type progression in the

Ex. 11. Mozart, Piano Concerto K. 491, Finale

[6] *Ibid., Anhang,* Fig. 154/4, p. 114.
[7] *Ibid., Anhang,* Fig. 21, p. 8.

immediate foreground of the first two bars. By contrast, the more background V in bar 4 involves a cadence which tonicizes V.

The above remarks represent only the lightest skimming over of a very complicated subject—especially since I have limited the discussion to dominant chords, to the exclusion of other common linear-chords* (p. 32). The reader will understand that to specify all the techniques for differentiating levels in the tonal system would go far beyond the compass of this study. I should add that since there are numerous criteria for determining the content of structural levels, there is no certainty that all the criteria in a given context will agree or that every context can be unequivocally analyzed into one set of levels.

'Higher' and 'prior' are synonyms for 'more background'; its antonyms are 'lower' and 'subsequent.' 'Prior' is to be differentiated from 'preceding,' which refers to an earlier time; and in the same way, 'subsequent' is to be differentiated from 'succeeding." Thus, one speaks of a "preceding time-span," meaning one that occurs at an earlier time-point in a given context; while one cites a "prior time-span" to indicate a time-span at a more background level.

2. Operation

A means for elaborating a given note configuration. There are two basic types of operations: 1) 'rhythmic operations,' which shift attack-points and/or alter the number of note-attacks in a given context; and 2) 'tonal operations,' which replace notes in given time-spans with notes of different pitch, in addition to altering rhythmic configurations.

Tonal operations provide 'linear connections' between pairs of notes generated at a higher level. If these notes are adjacent in a diatonic scale, the new 'linear-note' is a chromatic 'passing-note.' If the two given notes are members of the same pitch-class, the new linear-note is either a diatonic or a chromatic 'neighbor-note.' (The term 'linear-note' is useful for referring to a note as a linear connection without specifying precisely whether it is a passing-note or neighbor-note.) If the two notes are non-adjacent in a diatonic scale, the single or several new linear-notes are either diatonic or chromatic passing-notes. Passing-notes can fill in any diatonic interval, but there is a possibility of some confusion with intervals larger than a third, since some of the passing-notes could be interpreted as arpeggiation-notes* (p. 23), see Ex. 12. A neighbor prolongation

Ex. 12

need not be complete, but may start or end with the neighbor. (A passing-note prolongation is always understood to be complete.)

(In general, the term 'prolongation' refers to a collection of notes grouped at some level by virtue of the application of an operation to a prior configuration. 'Configuration' refers to groups of notes more generally, where some operational inter-relationship is presumed, but without specific reference to a prior configuration from which they are derived. Also, a configuration may be an individual chord or a horizontal grouping, whereas a prolongation is essentially just a succession of notes or chords. A 'passage' is generally simply a portion of an actual piece of music.)

The generation of a linear-note presupposes the prior generation of an 'arpeggiation-note(s)' to which it is linearly related. The arpeggiation-note operation is basically a rhythmic operation which replaces the attack of one note or the simultaneous attack of two or more notes with two or more successive note-attacks within the prior time-span of the given note(s). The simplest case of arpeggiation arises where two chord members which occupy the same time-span at one level are placed in successive portions of that time-span at the next subsequent level, as in Exx. 13a and b. Strictly speaking, exact repetition is

Ex. 13   Ex. 14

a result of arpeggiation, too (Exx. 14a and b). (The repeated notes are known as 'common-tones' with respect to one another.)

Two notes related by virtue of arpeggiation differ from two linearly related notes, in that at a prior level the two arpeggiation-notes are taken to be present throughout the total of their combined foreground time-spans, while one member of a linear-pair is always regarded as newly generated. (But not all scalar adjacencies are linear-pairs; see p. 41, below.) However, in a secondary sense, arpeggiation can be seen as a tonal operation, as in Ex. 15b where the bass F is newly generated in support of the soprano F. Although the bass F is essentially a linear-note which is not present at a prior level (Ex. 15a), one neverthe-

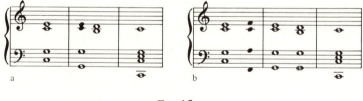

Ex. 15

less speaks of the arpeggiation of the bass interval, C-F, in Ex. 15b. Furthermore, in background contexts, one can generate a bass linear-note, and subsequently arpeggiate an interval from the triad of which the bass note is root—again without necessarily showing the arpeggiated triadic notes at a higher level (see the arpeggiated soprano interval, E♭-A♭, in Ex. 16b). For analytic purposes, notes are generally regarded as related by arpeggiation only when they occur in the same part* (p. 40);

Ex. 16

thus, in Ex. 15b, the bass notes C and F form an arpeggiated interval, whereas the first alto C and soprano F do not, by virtue of belonging to different parts.

As a purely rhythmic operation, arpeggiation usually involves the supression of one note in the latter portion of its prior time-span, in conjunction with the suppression of another note in the initial portion of the same time-span—as in Ex. 13. The attack-point of the first arpeggiation-note remains unaltered, but the attack-point of the second note is 'delayed.' Delay may occur independently, as in the case of the arpeggiation operation, or in conjunction with the substitution of a linear predisplacement* (p. 39) in the initial portion of the prior time-span of the delayed note. If the linear predisplacement is newly generated, it is called an 'appoggiatura,' or 'accented linear-note,' representing the combination of a tonal operation with a rhythmic operation. If the predisplacement is already present at a prior level, its extension is called a 'suspension.'[8] The displacement of a suspension is called a

---

[8] A suspension may resemble an appoggiatura if the predisplacement is subsequently suppressed in the latter part of its prior time-span. See Chapter Four, Section 2,A and Chapter Five, Section 3,A, below.
The typical harmony and counterpoint textbook instructs a student to resolve a suspension by step, as if the suspension arises first and then a suitable resolution for it is to be found. According to my view, the resolution arises first, and the suspension is generated at a subsequent level. This view is expressed by Fux in *Gradus ad Parnassum:* "The notes held over ... are nothing but retardations of the notes following.... [One] can see that it is easy to find the consonance into which any dissonance must resolve; that is to say, it must be resolved to the consonance which would occur on the downbeat of the following measure if the retardation were removed." Cf. Alfred Mann's English edition, *op. cit.,* p. 56; see also Ex. 1, p. 13, above.

'resolution,'[9] and in its prior time-span, the predisplacement is called a 'preparation.' If a note is attacked preceding its prior attack-point, the new part of the note is called an 'anticipation.' Two other sets of rhythmic operations, 'contraction'-'expansion,' and 'elision'-'bifurcation' (known collectively as the 'alteration' operations) are described in Chapter Three, Section 5.

All operations, tonal and rhythmic, involve 1) the suppression of a previously generated note during part of its prior time-span, and 2) the attack of some other note of the same or different pitch in its place. Suppression can also be applied independently without the substitution of a new note; this amounts to replacing part or even all of the time-span of the given note with silence, usually notated as a rest.[10] Example 17

Ex. 17

<hr />

[9] This definition of 'resolution' is to be differentiated from the other, more general definition of that term which applies to any note which displaces a dissonance. In fact, the resolution of a suspension may be *more* dissonant than the suspension; see "The consonant suspension," pp. 84-86, below.

[10] For examples of completely suppressed notes, see Chapter Five, pp. 132-133, below.

illustrates partial suppression (and delay) in connection with various configurations resulting from tonal and rhythmic operations.

In general, configurations resulting from tonal operations do not duplicate configurations which can be generated by means of rhythmic operations, and vice versa. Assuming Ex. 18

Ex. 18

represents the soprano line in a polyphonic context, D can arise in the first place as a passing-note at the fourth beat, or it can occur as the resolution of a suspension introduced at the third beat. Ordinarily the concurrence of other notes differentiates a linear-note from a resolution. In Ex. 19, D is attacked as a

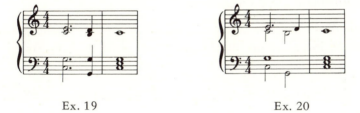

Ex. 19   Ex. 20

passing-note conjointly with other members of the dominant triad, whereas in Ex. 20, D is attacked independently as the resolution of a suspension. It would be inappropriate to describe Ex. 19 as a suspension configuration, or to describe Ex. 20 as a configuration resulting merely from a tonal operation. The difference in the two passages hinges upon the different kind of harmonic support* (p. 31) provided for the respective E's (at the third beat). (Harmonic support is one of the principal analytic criteria by which suspensions are differentiated from other types of notes; this subject is discussed in Chapter Four, Section 1, B, iii and in Chapter Five, Section 1, B, iv.)

Finally, I should point out that the term 'linear-note' is an abbreviation for "a linear-note at some level." At some other, lower, level the very same note may be regarded as an arpeggiation-note. For example, let us say that a passing-note, D, is generated between two arpeggiation-notes, E and C, and let us say that D is supported in a G major triad. At a subsequent level, a passing-note, C, may be generated between D and B of the G major triad. Now D, which was formerly called a linear-note, is now properly called an arpeggiation-note. It is still a linear-note with respect to E and C, between which two notes it passes; but it is also an arpeggiation-note with respect to the C which passes from it to B. By the same token, a suspension is necessarily not a common-tone at the level at which it arises; but it can be divided at a lower level into two (or more) attacks, in which case the second part of the suspension is a common-tone with respect to the first part.

3. Consonance and Dissonance

Qualities of an interval calculated according to the arrangement of intervals in Ex. 21. The first unit (a) consists of the

Ex. 21

unison; the second unit (b) contains the three intervals of the root-position major-minor triad, while the third unit (c) contains the inversions of these intervals. The fourth unit (d) consists of other intervals: diminished and augmented skips, as well as diatonic steps. (But not all notational possibilities of these intervals are included in the example.)

The simple intervals shown in Ex. 21 are intended to stand for their compound equivalents. Thus, the first unit includes octaves, the second unit perfect 12ths, etc.

An interval in any of the first three units is 'absolutely consonant,' and an interval in the fourth unit is 'absolutely

dissonant.' An absolutely consonant interval is 'relatively consonant' with respect to any interval placed to its right in the
example, and is correspondingly 'relatively dissonant' with
respect to any interval to its left. Absolutely dissonant intervals
are neither relatively consonant nor dissonant with respect to
each other, but are relatively dissonant with respect to any
absolutely consonant interval. Depending upon the verbal context, a 'consonant note' is simply a note which forms an
absolutely consonant interval with respect to some other note
—known as a 'reference-note'—in a pertinent time-span, or is a
note which is relatively more consonant with respect to some
reference-note than some other note with respect to the same or
a different reference-note. Thus, in Ex. 22, the soprano D is

Ex. 22   Ex. 23

consonant in the absolute sense, since it forms an octave with
the bass reference-note, D; it is also relatively consonant
compared to the notes E and F♯ with respect to the same
reference-note. F♯ is relatively dissonant compared to D,
relatively consonant compared to E, and absolutely consonant
in itself—all references being made to the bass D.

The principle of relative consonance and dissonance is useful
in contexts where root-position triadic support is replaced by
relatively less consonant inversionally triadic support (see p.
30). In Ex. 23, the soprano E is more consonant over the bass C
than over the bass G, although both reference-intervals are
absolutely consonant; this means that the absolutely consonant
E can nevertheless be analyzed as a dissonant suspension at the
third beat.[11] (The significance of the harmonic context of
suspensions is explained in Chapter Four, Section 1, B.)

[11]   See p. 31, below, for further discussion of Ex. 23.

The ordering within the second and third units of Ex. 21 is determined by the following considerations: a perfect fifth uniquely indicates a major or minor triad, whereas a major or minor third belongs to more than one such 'tonic-type' triad; therefore, the fifth is the more "stable" inverval. (Consonance is equated with stability and dissonance with instability.) The major third is considered more consonant than the minor third due to the primacy of the major mode in the tonal system.

As a group, the inversionally triadic intervals are not as stable as the root-position intervals, insofar as the lower note in each case cannot be a root or tonic to the upper note. The ordering within the third unit reverses that of the second unit; i.e., the inversion of the perfect fifth comes last, etc. This ordering is based upon the notion that inversion involves a change in quality from consonance to dissonance but preserves the quantitative relationships within a unit: thus, the perfect fifth is the most consonant interval in unit two (Ex. 21) and correspondingly inverts to the most dissonant interval in unit three.

4. Support

Pertains to the appropriateness of the presence of a note at some level. Thus, at a background level, a well-supported note appears more appropriately than a comparatively weakly supported note. Consonance and dissonance are among the principal criteria by which support is judged: consonance is characteristic of the background, while dissonance is more characteristic of the foreground. The soprano D of Ex. 24 is

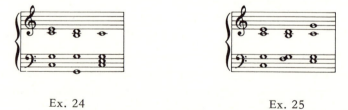

Ex. 24   Ex. 25

better supported than the soprano D of Ex. 25, since a perfect fifth is more consonant than a major sixth; consequently, the

harmonic context of D in Ex. 25 is appropriate to a foreground level, while the support for D in Ex. 24 is more suitable
for the background. (As I have already indicated in the
discussion of levels, remarks of this sort are meant to be
suggestive rather than binding.)

The term 'harmonic support' refers to support provided for
higher-pitched notes by lower-pitched notes. Generally, harmonic support is judged by the most dissonant reference-
interval, whenever a given note occurs in conjunction with more
than one reference-note (as in a block chord). In Ex. 23, the
interval formed between the second soprano E and the alto C is
more consonant than the interval between the following D and
B; nevertheless, the second E is not as strongly supported as D,
because the interval G-E is more dissonant than G-D and B-D.
Between two notes which form the same set of reference-
intervals (or their equivalents, modulo 7), a comparison is based
on the reference-intervals formed with the relevant *bass* notes.
Thus, in Ex. 23 the second E is given weaker harmonic support
than the first E—although both E's have equivalent sets of
reference-intervals—because G-E is more dissonant than C-E.

In a polyphonic context, the generation of a foreground
linear-note may result in a chord consisting (in addition to the
linear-note) of prior notes from the time-span of the linear-note.
Thus, in Ex. 26, the newly generated passing-note, D, forms a

Ex. 26

dissonant chord with the other (prior) notes occupying its
time-span, C and G. At background and middleground levels,
however, linear-notes are generated with consonant harmonic
support, as I have already indicated in the discussion of levels,
pp. 17-19, above. A chord which is introduced specifically to
provide consonant support for a linear-note is known as a

'linear-chord.' The V chord in Ex. 27 is just such a linear-chord; indeed, any non-tonic chord containing a supported linear-note

Ex. 27

is a linear-chord. Of course, linear-chords which arise at a background or middleground level are typically arpeggiated, as the foundation for the generation of more foreground linear-chords. In order to differentiate between the structural function of a chord which arises linearly at one level and is subsequently arpeggiated at a lower level, I call the given chord a linear-chord with respect to the 'arpeggiation-chords' between which its linear-notes are generated; and I then call the given chord an arpeggiation-chord with respect to the more foreground linear-notes for which it provides an arpeggiated foundation. (See the discussion of the generation of linear-notes, p. 23, above.)

There are numerous criteria for determining support other than consonance and dissonance, and it is not unusual to regard a relatively dissonant note as better supported than a given note on account of some of these criteria. Among them are the number of pitch changes which occur simultaneously in other parts* (p. 40) in conjunction with the attack of a given note, and the presence or absence of accompanying bass motion, in particular. Thus, the neighbor-note F in Ex. 28 is better

Ex. 28

supported than the relatively consonant F in Ex. 29, due to the fact that the former F is accompanied by corresponding pitch

Ex. 29

displacements in all the other parts, while the latter F is accompanied by only one such displacement (not occurring in the bass part). Example 29 represents a pedal configuration—one having no bass motion—one of the most typical of foreground chordal configurations. All the same, bass motion does not always outweigh consonance, as a comparison of Exx. 29 and 30 shows; for the F in the pedal configuration is unquestionably

Ex. 30

better supported than the F in Ex. 30. An upper-part arpeggiation-note is better supported if accompanied by a corresponding bass motion than if a preceding bass note is maintained throughout the time-span in question (see Exx. 31a and b, respectively). Also, the repetition of the bass note counts for more than non-repetition (see Exx. 31c and b, respectively).

Ex. 31

Another criterion of support is register. The lower of two octave representations of the same pitch-class would generally be regarded as providing better bass support than the higher one. Similarly, membership in the soprano part confers stronger support upon a given note than does membership in an inner part, unless dynamics or other factors offset this effect.

Support in a tonic triad is generally superior to other consonant triadic support. In Ex. 32, the soprano E♭ of bar 5 is

Ex. 32. Chopin, Etude Op. 10/6 [reduced]

more consonant (in an A♭ minor 6/3 chord) than the initial soprano G♭, since the intervals C♭-E♭ and A♭-E♭ are more consonant than E♭-G♭ and B♭-G♭; but G♭ draws support as the melodic member of the foreground tonic triad, and is therefore better supported than E♭, which appears melodically only in a non-tonic (IV) chord. Furthermore, G♭ is also better supported as a melodic note than the other tonic member, B♭, because B♭ appears in the soprano part exclusively as a member of non-tonic harmonies.

Also, the notes of a given chord appearing in a foreground prolongation of that chord are better supported, by virtue of their outside positioning in that prolongation, than the notes of the other, "inside" chords therein. Thus, in Ex. 33, the soprano

Ex. 33

D's are more strongly supported than the relatively consonant soprano E♭, since they are located in the outside chords of that prolongation (of the B♭ chord). Positioning is an effective criterion of support, even where the prolonged background chord is dissonant, as in Ex. 34. The conflict between these two

Ex. 34

criteria—positioning and harmonic support—accounts to some degree for the relative unsuitability of dissonant chords for prolongation; the resulting linear (inside)-chord tends to be more consonant than the supposedly more stable outer chords. Passages of this sort occur, nevertheless, with considerable frequency at foreground and middleground levels (see Ex. 35), and in such cases the prolonged dissonant chord is analogous to a local tonic in spite of its dissonance.

Ex. 35. Schubert, Symphony in C (D. 944), Finale

Rhythmic effects—especially metrical accent and duration—play an important role in determining support. But since both the suspension and the appoggiatura are normally metrically accented with respect to their displacements (regarding suspensions, see Chapter Three, Section 6, pp. 67-69), it follows that metrical accent is not a safe indicator of the level priority of one note with respect to another. Also, a suspension or appoggiatura may have a greater duration than its displacement, in spite of the level priority of its displacement.

There are numerous other criteria of support which I shall not attempt to list here.

5. Time-Span

A musical continuum may be likened to a straight line: it consists of an ordered set of 'time-points,' infinite in number. A 'time-span' is a portion of a musical continuum between two time-points. It may be thought of simply as a musical distance, represented notationally as a portion of music between two time-points. Note that a time-span is not a portion of time, but rather the location of part or all of a piece of music. Such locations may be identified in relation to other time-spans, as in Ex. 36b, where D can be said to occupy the second half (not just any half)[12] of the time-span between E and C; or they may be identified in notational terms, as where D, in the same example, is said to be located in the second half of bar 1. (For further discussion of time-span locations, see Chapter Three, Section 1.)

Ex. 36

A note may occupy different time-spans at different levels; a note generated at one level may, at a subsequent level, occupy part of its prior time-span, or that time-span exactly, or an adjacent time-span in addition to part or all of its own prior time-span, or none of that time-span—as, e.g., in the case of total suppression (see Chapter Five, Section 2, D). In Ex. 36b, E occupies just the first half of its prior time-span (Ex. 36a). In cases where a prior note is simply divided into self-repetitions at a lower level, one can say that the given note (*qua* pitch-class) occupies a cumulative time-span which is unchanged from its prior level, while acknowledging that no longer just one note,

---

[12] It would be misleading and inaccurate to say simply that D occupies one-half the prior time-span of E, since the boundary time-points of the time-span of D are not thereby identified. On the other hand, one could say without further qualification that D has a duration equal to half the prior duration of E. See the discussion of duration, p. 37 below.

but several notes (known as 'common-tones') are present, each occupying a portion of the prior time-span of the undivided note. This effect is illustrated in Ex. 37. The notion of a single

Ex. 37. Beethoven, Piano Sonata Op. 53, 1st movement

note having different time-spans at different levels is particularly useful in speaking of suspensions and resolutions; for one says of a suspension that it occupies an initial portion of the prior time-span of its resolution, while the latter occupies only the remaining portion of that prior time-span.

The term 'duration' differs from 'time-span,' insofar as two notes of the same duration may occupy different time-spans (E and D in Ex. 36b). Furthermore, the same note may occupy different time-spans at different levels and yet retain the same duration (E and D in Exx. 36b and c). The notion of duration approaches that of a portion of time; but, practically speaking, duration depends upon performance, so that in saying that two notes have the same duration, one can only mean approximately the same (which includes the possibility of exactly the same—the point being that traditionally there has been no precise control).

An 'attack-point' is the initial time-point of a note's time-span at some level. The attack-point of a given note may be shifted at subsequent levels; and thus a note may have a set of different attack-points at a number of corresponding levels. Let me emphasize that the term 'attack-point' merely means the initial time-point of a time-span *at some level,* and does not necessarily refer to the actual foreground location of a note-attack, unless specifically or contextually so indicated.

Just as an attack-point marks the beginning of a time-span, a 'discontinuation-point' marks its end. In the absolute foreground, the articulation of a given note, i.e., the period of its actual sounding, lasts quite literally from its foreground attack-point to its foreground discontinuation-point. However, a note may appear to occupy a foreground time-span which continues beyond its foreground discontinuation-point in certain cases where that discontinuation-point precedes the foreground attack-point of the note's 'linear displacement'* (p. 39). In Ex. 38b, E is discontinued at the second beat, but appears to

Ex. 38

occupy a time-span lasting until the third beat, since the attack-point of its linear displacement, D, does not actually occur until that time-point. This foreground configuration is derived from the prior configuration in Ex. 38a, where the discontinuation and linear displacement of E occur simultaneously, i.e., where E explicitly lasts for two beats.

6. Linear Relationships

A linear-note may occupy either the beginning or ending of the prior time-span of some arpeggiation-note. In the latter case the linear-note is unaccented (Ex. 39b), whereas in the former it

Ex. 39

is known as accented (Ex. 39c) and also as an appoggiatura. An accented linear-note delays the attack of the arpeggiation-note in the time-span of which it is generated. Where two or more passing-notes are generated, it is possible for the new configuration to have both accented and unaccented passing-notes (Ex. 40).

Ex. 40

The linear-notes portrayed in Exx. 39 and 40 are notated as actual pitch connections between registrally close arpeggiation-notes. It is not my intention, however, to limit the notion of a linear-note to pitch connections. A linear-note is basically a *pitch-class* connection, which may or may not appear in the same register as the arpeggiation-note(s) which it adjoins. In Ex. 41, I regard the left-hand G as a neighbor-note to F, although the pitches F and G happen to lie in different octaves.

Ex. 41. Beethoven, Piano Sonata
Op. 10/3, 2nd movement

The second note of a 'linear-pair'* (p. 14) is considered the 'stepwise displacement' (or simply, 'displacement') of the first note, and the first note is called the 'predisplacement' of the second note. The two members of a linear-pair are said to be in the same 'voice.' A note may be the first note of two linear-pairs, with simultaneous or successive displacement in two directions (Ex. 42); also, a note may be held in one voice

Ex. 42   Ex. 43

while being displaced in another (Ex. 43). Therefore, while the displacement of a note represents its discontinuation in one voice, it does not preclude its continuation in another voice. The term 'displacement' refers to the succession of the first note of a linear-pair by the second note, as well as to that second note itself.

The terms 'part' and 'voice' are to be distinguished from each other. In Ex. 44, F, G♯, and A are all in the soprano part,

Ex. 44

but F is in one voice, while G♯ and A are in another. 'Part' is a registral term: there are as many parts in a given time-span as there are different notes simultaneously articulated in that time-span. (A note which subsequently displaces or is displaced by two different notes is often notated as a unison and considered to represent two parts.) The soprano part consists of the highest notes in successive time-spans, and the bass part consists of the lowest notes in successive time-spans.[13] Two notes in the same voice may or may not be in the same part, and two notes in the same part may or may not be in the same voice. Thus, in Ex. 45, E and D are in the same voice, but not

Ex. 45

the same part; E and G are in the same part, but not in the same voice; and F and E are in the same part *and* voice. F and G are not in the same voice, because F is resolved to E before G is attacked. The final C is in the same parts as both D and G, but is in the same voice as D alone.

According to customary usage, one speaks of all the members of a sequence of linear-pairs—in which the first note of one linear-pair is the second note of a preceding linear-pair—as if they belonged to the same voice. Thus, two notes which

[13] In choral music, however, the notes assigned to sopranos may occasionally cross below the notes assigned to altos, etc. Since I deal almost exclusively with instrumental passages in this book, the term 'soprano' always means 'highest part.'

represent two voices at one level (Ex. 46) may become osten-
sible members of the "same" voice at a subsequent level (Ex.47)

Ex. 46   Ex. 47

by virtue of a passing-note newly generated between them. This
usage is accepted here, but the customary interchange of the
terms 'part' and 'voice' is not. This obviates the necessity of
having to say that two notes in the same voice, i.e., in the same
registral part, are not in the same voice, i.e., are not members
of a single linear-pair.

Observe that two notes of adjacent pitch in adjacent time-
spans do not necessarily form a linear-pair. Thus, in Ex. 48a, the

Ex. 48a

C♯ and C♮ of bar 2 are passing-notes from the pitch-class D in
bar 1, but are not linearly related to the D in bar 2 (Ex. 48b).

Ex. 48b. Mozart, Piano Sonata K. 545, 1st movement, bars 12-14

Even where three succeeding scalar adjacencies are present in
the same part, the middle note need not always be regarded as
linearly related to both the outer notes. Thus, in Ex. 44, G♯ is

not a passing-note between F and A. By the same token, the presence of two notes of adjacent pitch in *different* parts does not necessarily negate a linear connection; in Ex. 49, the soprano B♭ of bar 1 passes from the initial soprano C to the alto A♭ of bar 2.

Ex. 49. Beethoven, Piano Sonata Op. 13, 2nd movement

A note may displace a note occupying a preceding adjacent time-span, even where the earlier note is not generated in connection with the later note. Thus, in Ex. 50, the bass note G

Ex. 50

represents the stepwise displacement of the bass note F, although the latter is generated primarily as triadic support for the soprano note F, rather than as a linear-note associated with the bass note, G.

The temporal adjacency of a linear-pair at its original level is not invariably retained in the foreground; but the two notes are still regarded as a (large-scale) linear-pair. In certain cases (as described above pp. 37-38), the prior adjacency of the two time-spans appears retained in the foreground, in spite of the literal separation.

Also, it should be made clear that a note may have various linear displacements at various levels. Very fast, unsupported displacements tend not to obscure supported prior linear connections; but supported middleground linear connections tend to make still more background linear connections difficult to assay.

A caret (⌃) above an Arabic numeral is shorthand for the expression 'scale-degree' preceding the numeral. Roman numerals also refer to scale-degrees, but the two types of numerals are used in different verbal contexts. A Roman numeral suggests a triad constructed on a given root, which is a member of a scale of some tonic. An Arabic numeral below a bass note signifies the diatonic interval between some member of that chord and the bass note; while an Arabic numeral under a caret is used to refer to the scale-degree of a note within the "horizontal'" domain of a given tonic. In Ex. 51 E is the 6th

Ex. 51

scale-degree of G♯ minor, as well as the root of an E major triad. Both the Roman and Arabic numerals, VI and 6, refer to G♯ as tonic (I), although the upper-part E is obviously $\hat{8}$ (or $\hat{1}$) with respect to VI (E). But only $\hat{6}$ is written above E, to signify its relationship to the tonic G♯. Thus, there is an important distinction between the use of Arabic numerals in expressions like "V 5/3" and "2/V" (Ex. 52): the "5" in the first

Ex. 52

expression refers to the A♯ a fifth above a root which is understood *not* to be the basic tonic; the "2" refers to the same A♯ as the second scale-degree of the basic tonic (G♯).

7. Suspension Configuration

A configuration consisting of 1) a preparation, suspension, and resolution in successive adjacent time-spans, and 2) one or more reference-notes* (page 29) occupying those time-spans. A suspension would not occur in a one-part texture, since the identical rhythmic configuration could be generated more simply without a subsequent additional shifting operation. Thus, in Ex. 53, there is no point in first generating E as a half-note and then suspending it; it can be generated as a dotted half-note to begin with.

Ex. 53

A suspension and its resolution invariably form a linear-pair —as opposed to an arpeggiated skip—at the level at which the suspension is generated. The source of the linear aspect of suspension configurations lies in a fundamental aspect of the tonal system: the different rhythmic implications of an arpeggiated skip and a linear succession. To begin with, a suspension is understood to be an extension of one note into the time-span of another note, effecting a delay in the attack of the second note. Now in order for a note to be a suspension, it must appear to be newly generated in its time-span; and similarly the resolution must appear to be newly deferred from the present attack-point of the suspension. The suspension is present at that attack-point at one level, and the resolution is located there at a prior level; but there is *no* level at which both notes are present at that attack-point *simultaneously*. However, *both members* of an arpeggiated skip normally occupy their total time-span at a prior level (see pp. 23-25, above). Therefore, the first member of such a skip can hardly be regarded as an extension at the level of the arpeggiation; it was already present there at a prior level. (But cf. Chapter Five, Section 2, C, i for a context in which a suspension chord itself is arpeggiated.) Moreover, the resolution of a suspension is delayed in conjunction with the generation of the suspension; but the second note of an arpeggiation cannot be regarded as delayed in conjunction with the generation of the first note—again since they are both normally present throughout their total time-span at a prior level.

In contrast to arpeggiation-pairs, both members of a linear adjacency would not ordinarily be found jointly occupying a prior time-span (although this is not an impossibility, see p. 41, above). Thus, while the succession C-E-G represents an arpeggiation which reduces at a prior level to a block chord consisting of these three non-adjacent scale-degrees, the succession C-D-E does not correspondingly reduce to a block chord consisting of three adjacent scale-degrees. Instead, at least one of the three notes would appear to be a foreground linear connection and would not show up in a background sketch. And so it is entirely possible for that linear connection to be generated at the prior attack-point of its displacement; where D is the linear connection, it can be generated at the prior attack-point of E, with the consequent delay in the attack of E. In this case, D is an appoggiatura; in the case where it is first generated as an unaccented passing-note in the prior time-span of C and subsequently extended into the time-span of E, D is a suspension.

In sum, a linear succession carries the potential (but not necessary) implication of delay in the attack of the second note *in conjunction with* the generation of the first note; an arpeggiated skip carries the potential (but not necessary) implication of delay in the attack of the second note *independent of* the generation of the first note.

Of course, other elements must be present in a configuration if one is to regard the first member of a linear-pair as a suspension. One of these elements is the metrical positions of the two linear-notes with respect to each other; I shall reserve discussion of this aspect of suspension configurations for Chapter Three. The other element is the harmonic context. The first note of a linear-pair can ordinarily be regarded as a suspension only if it occurs successively at some level in two different harmonies, where the remaining notes of the second harmony are associated with the support of the second note of the given linear-pair. Thus, in Ex. 54, E is a common-tone and

Ex. 54

not a suspension at the third beat, for the remaining notes at that beat are associated with the support of E rather than D. On the other hand, D *is* a suspension in bar 2, because it occurs in conjunction with members of the background C major triad to which its linear displacement—namely, C—belongs. A very important principle is involved here: notes which support a given note may remain in the original time-span of that note even when that note is subsequently shifted into a different time-span.

Finally, how are we to account for a note which appears successively as a consonance and then a dissonance, but has no apparent linear resolution? In Ex. 55, E sounds like a

Ex. 55

suspension, but C is ruled out as its resolution, in accordance with the idea that a suspension does not resolve by skip. That C is not a resolution seems reasonable, since it is present along with E in the IV7 chord, and therefore is not delayed by E. On the other hand, I would not want to regard E as a common-tone at beat 3 (for reasons presented in Chapter Five, Section 3, C). In this case, I would regard E as a suspension which resolves to F in another register. Similarly, B is not the resolution of E in Ex. 56; rather, B resolves an 'implied' suspension (see Chapter

Ex. 56

V, Section 2, D, iii), C, while E is resolved to the explicit F (and implied D) of the V chord, again in a different register.

We have been talking about suspensions followed by skips in conjunction with linear resolutions in other registers. In addition, it is not at all uncommon to find a suspension which is resolved by step in the same register, but which is separated from that resolution due to the interpolation of subsequently generated notes. However, the original temporal adjacency of suspension and resolution often remains transparent in such foreground contexts, especially in cases where the suspension remains undisplaced by the more foreground notes. A typical example would arise when an entire suspension chord is arpeggiated before the attack of the resolution (Ex. 57). This

Ex. 57

transparency is analogous to that of a background bass note carried down into the foreground as a pedal point; in both cases, the foreground elaborations fail to obscure the prior rhythmic relationships.

CHAPTER THREE

METER AND THE SUSPENSION

In order to specify the metrical characteristics of the suspension, one must have recourse to a formulated theory of meter. Since I have not encountered a satisfactory theory of meter—one that integrates metrical values with pitch values rather than treating meter as an independent aspect of music—I shall present an original formulation here. I proceed upon the assumption that a theory of meter should fulfill two requirements. 1) It should provide for the derivation of metrical values through a set of structural levels, analogous to Schenker's theory of pitch derivation. And 2), the operations for deriving metrical values should be the same as, or at least coordinated with, the operations for deriving pitches. The theory is presented in Sections 1-5, below, followed by a description of the metrical characteristics of the suspension in Section 6 and a summary in Section 7.

1. Background Time-Spans

We are quite used to the idea of an 'eight-bar phrase,' meaning a phrase occupying a time-span measured as eight bars from its attack-point to its discontinuation-point. We can observe an eight-bar phrase in Ex. 58, and also notice that the phrase is subdivided into two four-bar halves. However, there is something peculiarly unbalanced about this apparently square-cut phrase: it ends at the end of the eighth bar, but its authentic cadence occurs at the middle of that bar (with the attack of the root position I triad). Moreover, the preceding V cadence occurs at the middle of bar 4, so that the time-span between the opening of the phrase and the V cadence (three and a half bars) is shorter than the time-span between the V cadence and the I cadence (four bars). Indeed, the time-span between the opening tonic downbeat and the final tonic cadential attack is measured as just *seven and a half* bars, not eight.

49

Ex. 58. Mozart, Piano Sonata K. 331, 1st movement

The general problem confronting us here is determining what counts as the end of a phrase or other unit of music. In one sense, the phrase in Ex. 58 ends at the end of the eighth bar (or rather at the beginning of the ninth bar); but in another sense, it ends with the cadence at the middle of that bar—since, after all, the term 'cadence' refers to an ending. As a solution to this problem, I offer the notion of a 'structural time-span,' which ends at the cadence of a phrase or other unit. Thus, the time-span of a final cadential chord(s) lies outside the structural time-span of a given unit, while still belonging to that unit. (I should add that just as the structural ending of a unit need not coincide with its discontinuation-point, its structural beginning may not coincide with its attack-point. I discuss this matter further in the Appendix.)

When we consider the time-span of the ultimate (first) background level of a piece, we are faced with a unique situation. At that level, there is just one tonic attack (see Ex. 59a), so the time-span at that level has a discontinuation-point

Ex. 59

but no structural ending corresponding to a cadence. At the next level, however, the tonic is attacked twice (Ex. 59b); now there is an attack-point (the attack-point of the second tonic) which can serve as the cadential time-point of the structural time-span of the entire piece. The second tonic at this level has an independent time-span that resembles (in its independence) the time-span of the cadential tonic in the second half of bar 8, Ex. 58. The time-span of the second tonic at level two lies outside the background structural time-span and is reserved for foreground prolongations which would comprise a 'coda' or its equivalent.

The background structural time-span can be located at the second and subsequent levels as falling between the two tonic attack-points at the penultimate background level; but the actual duration of this time-span has not been specified. In the foreground of the piece, the actual approximate duration of the background structural time-span will amount to the cumulation of the durations of the successive notes and rests generated within that time-span. (The conditions under which these notes and rests are generated are outlined in the remainder of this chapter.)

I should add that my view of the first two background levels differs from Schenker's, inasmuch as I conceive of them as primarily harmonic, while he viewed the background as an essentially two-part contrapuntal structure.[1] This difference need not obtrude for those who subscribe to his or other views of the background; for my theories about meter and time-spans at various levels can be coordinated with any particular view of the pitch-class or pitch content of these levels.

2. Background Meter

The generation of one or more notes into equal subdivisions of the background structural time-span provides the initial articulation of meter. Let us assume that this time-span is sub-

---

[1] Cf. *Der freie Satz, Anhang*, Fig. 1, p. 1.

divided into *n* equal portions, where *n* is a whole number greater than 1. Defining 'beat' as the initial time-point of an equal sub-division of the background structural time-span, there are now *n* beats in that time span.

3. Meter at Subsequent Levels

The term 'beat' may be extended to include the initial time-point of any time-span which is an equal subdivision of a time-span the initial time-point of which is a beat (by virtue of prior equal subdivision of some larger time-span).[2] The beats at a given level are interrelated according to a hierarchy of 'metrical levels.' There are as many metrical levels in connection with a divisor *n* as there are members of a set of whole numbers which form a 'sequence of multiples' ending with *n*. A sequence of multiples is a set of numbers arranged from low to high; the first number is a prime number greater than 1; the second number is found by multiplying the first number by a prime number higher than 1; and each succeeding number in the set is similarly the result of multiplying the preceding number by a prime number higher than 1 (not necessarily the same prime number used to multiply other members of the set). Thus, where *n* = 4, there is a sequence of two multiples, 2 and 4. (See Section 4, A, below, for a discussion of cases where *n* is the final member of more than one sequence of multiples.) Where *n* = 2, the sequence consists of just one member, *n*. (See p. 54, below, for cases where *n* is a prime number higher than 2.)

Each member of a sequence of multiples indicates the number of beats at the metrical level to which it corresponds. Thus, where *n* = 4, the sequence of multiples, 2 and 4, indicates that there are two beats at the first or higher metrical level and four beats at the second, or lower, metrical level (see Ex. 60).

The concept of metrical levels is similar but not identical to the concept of structural levels. In Ex. 61 we find a foreground derivation involving one new structural level, and also one

---

[2] According to customary usage, the term 'beat' is also used to signify a time-span *between* two beats (i.e., between two time-points).

resultant metrical level. In Ex. 60 there is again just one new structural level, but *two* resultant metrical levels.

$N = 4$

𝅝

♩ ♩ ♩ ♩

$N = 2$

𝅝

♩ ♩

1st metrical level: 1   2
2nd metrical level: 1 2 3 4

1   2

Ex. 60   Ex. 61

The process of generating metrical levels in a given time-span involves selecting certain undifferentiated time-points as beats. For example, where $n = 2$, the second beat is present as an undifferentiated time-point at the prior structural level; the subdivision of the given time-span into two equal parts converts the initial time-point of the second part from an undifferentiated time-point into a beat. At the metrical level at which a time-point is converted into a beat, that beat is regarded as 'weak' with respect to any beat occurring within the given time-span at a higher metrical level. Thus, where $n = 4$, beat 2 is weak with respect to beats 1 and 3, which occur at the higher metrical level; similarly, beat 3 is weak with respect to beat 1 (to which it relates as beat 2 where $n = 2$). Conversely, 'strong' beats at a given metrical level are those which coincide with beats at a higher metrical level: other beats at the given metrical level are weak with respect to these beats. 'Strong' and 'weak,' then, are relational terms, since only the first beat at the first metrical level remains unchanged in quality at subsequent metrical levels; while all other beats are weak at higher metrical levels and strong at lower metrical levels. The interrelations of strong and weak beats at higher metrical levels carry down into lower metrical levels, so that in the foreground, beats are typically both strong and weak relative to different time-spans.

A strong beat does not ordinarily follow another strong beat at a given metrical level (the exception occurring in connection with the bifurcation operation; see pp. 62 and 66, below). Therefore, where n is greater than 2, there is ordinarily a series of alternating strong and weak beats, in which every strong beat is succeeded by a weak beat, and vice versa. Thus, a strong beat is strong not only with respect to a succeeding beat, but also with respect to a preceding adjacent beat which arises at a lower metrical level than the given beat. For example, the third beat of four is stronger than the second beat, as well as the fourth. A note located at a strong beat is 'metrically accented' with respect to a note located at a weak beat, and is 'metrically unaccented' with respect to a note located at a still stronger beat.

Where n is a prime number higher than 2, the hierarchy of metrical levels is similar to that of $n + 1$.[3] Thus, the third beat of three is stronger than the second beat, just like the third beat of four. Where $n = 5$, there are two metrical levels, corresponding to the multiples 2 and 6. At the second metrical level, the fourth beat is stronger than the third and fifth beats, but weaker than the first beat. Moreover, at any level at which a strong beat is followed by two weak beats, the second of the two weak beats is regarded as stronger than the first. Thus, where $n = 5$ or 6, the third beat is stronger than the second beat. However, the notion of strong-weak is somewhat less powerful in comparing two beats which are both weak with respect to an initial strong beat (due to subdivision by n, where n is a prime number greater than 2).

---

[3] In order to avoid unintended syncopated effects (see Section 4,B, below, for a discussion of syncopation), the first member of a sequence of multiples whose last member is prime and higher than 3 is 2. E.g., where $n = 5$ and the first member is 3, the third beat at the second metrical level would seem stronger than the fifth beat, since the fifth beat is curtailed. This would imply a first metrical level with just two notes, the second of larger duration than the first (beats 3-5 versus beats 1-2)—an example of syncopation. See Ex. 62.

Ex. 62

4. Metrical Constraints on Tonal and Rhythmic Operations

A. *General Considerations*

The set of metrical levels which arises in connection with the generation of a note in a given time-span governs the placement of further notes to be generated within that time-span. (See below for the case where more than one set of metrical levels occurs for a given *n*.) Where a given note is generated in the *n*th equal part of a given time-span, other notes can be subsequently generated only in portions of that time-span where the initial time-point and strongest beat thereof coincide. For example, in a case where *n* = 8, subsequent notes could be generated within the given time-span at the fifth beat (second beat at the first metrical level) and/or seventh beat (fourth beat at the second metrical level), at the third and fifth beats, or at all of the third, fifth, and seventh beats (see Ex. 63).

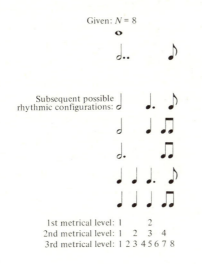

Ex. 63

On the other hand, a note would not be generated at other time-points in the given time-span, because the resulting metrical articulations would conflict with the metrical levels of the given time-span. For example, in Ex. 64b, bar 1, *n* = 4. The

Ex. 64

first note, E, occupies the initial three-fourths of its prior time-span, which is shown in Ex. 64a, bar 1. At the next level, an arpeggiation-note, C, is to be introduced between E and D. The divisor 2 is not feasible (see Ex. 65), since the resulting

Ex. 65

metrical articulation conflicts with the metrical articulation at the next prior level. Specifically, there is a problem at the third beat of bar 1. In Ex. 64b, the third beat represents the second strongest beat in the time-span of E. But in Ex. 65, the third beat is a mid-point in the time-span of the first C, i.e., the third beat is relatively weak with respect to the attack-point of C, which has now taken over the position as second strongest beat in the bar. Conversely, the second strongest beat in Ex. 65 (the fourth eighth-note) is a relatively weak beat in Ex. 64b. The conflict of meters is indicated by the fact that the three beats of Ex. 65 do not represent equal subdivisions of the entire bar.

A given n may be the final member of more than one sequence of multiples: thus, where $n = 6$, there are two sequences of multiples— 2,6 and 3,6; where $n = 12$, there are three sequences of multiples: 2,6,12; 2,4,12; and 3, 6, 12. More than one of these sequences may govern the placement of notes within a given time-span at subsequent levels. For example, with $n = 12$, the ninth beat may be strong with respect to the tenth beat at one metrical level, according to one sequence of multiples (3, 6, 12); while at the same time, the tenth beat may be strong with respect to the ninth beat at one metrical level, according to another sequence of multiples (2, 4, 12). Clearly the texture would consist of at least two parts, one representing each sequence of multiples. The resulting metrical mixture would represent a special case of 'joint meters,' rather than the counterpoint of one syncopated part against an unsyncopated part.

B. *The Rule of Syncopation*

'Syncopation' refers to a time-span which contains a stronger beat within it than at its beginning. We can infer from Section 4, A, that a note generated by virtue of a tonal or rhythmic operation occupies an original time-span which is unsyncopated; for it is only appropriate that at its original level a note's attack-point should coincide with the strongest time-point in its time-span. Example 65, an example of syncopation, is not an 'original' configuration; rather, it is derived from an unsyncopated configuration, such as Ex. 66.

Ex. 66

Syncopation, then, is a criterion of weak support, indicative of a relatively foreground level, and implying a more background level at which the given syncopated notes occur in unsyncopated time-spans.

Syncopation arises through the application of rhythmic operations which either extend a note backward or forward into an adjacent time-span (Exx. 67 and 68). Note that in Ex. 68b,

Ex. 67

the total time-span occupied by D is syncopated, although the time-span of each independently articulated D is unsyncopated. In describing a time-span as syncopated, the number of note-

Ex. 68

attacks within it is immaterial, although the relevance of such a description is usually limited to time-spans containing undisplaced notes, e.g., the soprano D in bars 1-2 of Ex. 68b.

Once a note is shifted into a syncopated time-span, operations can be applied in that time-span, providing that none of the one or more newly generated notes itself occupies a syncopated time-span. In Ex. 69c, the syncopated time-span of

Ex. 69

the first A♭ chord is divided by $n = 2$, in connection with the generation of the subsidiary 16 chord (Ex. 69d). Observe that the attack-point of the newly generated chord is already established as a (strong) beat at a higher metrical level.

C. *Specifics*

The generation of one or more notes by means of tonal and rhythmic operations involves the division of the time-span of a prior note into two or more equal unsyncopated parts, and the distribution of the foreshortened prior note and the new note(s) into these portions of the given time-span.

1. Where an operation produces just one new note, that note may occupy either an initial or final portion of the time-span of the background note.

a) In the event of a final portion, that portion is 1/nth of the original time-span, where n is any whole number above 1 with the exception of a prime number higher than 3, and providing that the resulting time-span is unsyncopated (see Ex. 70). Where n is a prime number higher than 3, the

e.g., n = 6

Ex. 70

unsyncopated time-span of the new note may be x/n (where x is 1 or a whole number higher than 1), but not more than ½ the original time-span (see note 3, p. 54, above, and Ex. 71). The background note then occupies the time-span from its prior initial attack-point to the attack-point of the new note.

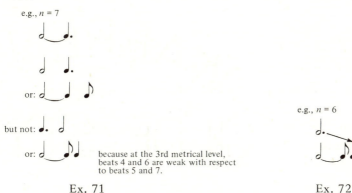

e.g., n = 7

or:

but not:

or:

because at the 3rd metrical level, beats 4 and 6 are weak with respect to beats 5 and 7.

Ex. 71

e.g., n = 6

Ex. 72

b) If the new note occupies an initial portion of the original time-span, the background note is assigned to a final nth of its original time-span (or a final x/nth of that time-span, where n is a prime number higher than 3, and providing that x/n equals less than ½), and the new note occupies the time-span from the prior attack-point of the background note to its new attack-point (see Ex. 72).

2. The generation of more than one new note involves any one of the following possibilities:

a) equal division of the time-span of the prior note by the number of new notes plus 1, with each note, including the prior note, occupying one of the resulting portions (independently) (see Ex. 73);

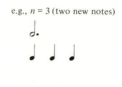

e.g., $n = 3$ (two new notes)

Ex. 73

b) duple division of the original time-span, with all the newly generated notes occupying equal subdivisions of the second half (see Ex. 74);

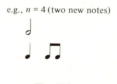

e.g., $n = 4$ (two new notes)

Ex. 74

c) where the number of new notes is odd, equal subdivision by that number, with the background and all but two of the notes occupying one resulting portion each, and the remaining two notes being assigned to equal subdivisions of the final portion (see Ex. 75);

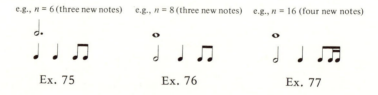

e.g., $n = 6$ (three new notes)   e.g., $n = 8$ (three new notes)   e.g., $n = 16$ (four new notes)

Ex. 75   Ex. 76   Ex. 77

d) a combination of b) and c), wherein the original time-span is divided in half, and the new notes occupy unequal portions of the second half (see Exx. 76 and 77);

e) other combinations of a similar nature.

3. A note once generated may be suppressed in some or all of its prior time-span independent of the generation of new notes in that time-span, under the following conditions.

a) If the suppression occurs in a final portion of the prior time-span, the constraints are the same as those under 1, a), above (see Ex. 78).

e.g., $n = 4$ or e.g., $n = 8$ e.g., $n = 2$

Ex. 78   Ex. 79

b) If the suppression occurs in an initial portion of the prior time-span, the constraints are the same as those under 1, b), above (see Ex. 79).

Note that in order to effect a syncopated time-span as the result of independent suppression, one would have to introduce at least one shifting operation. Thus to achieve an eighth-rest followed by a doubly dotted half-note in a 4/4 measure, one would proceed through the levels illustrated in Ex. 80. Observe

$n = 2$

$n = 2$

$n = 2$

Ex. 80

that an initial $n = 8$ is not possible, since a note cannot occupy a syncopated time-span at the level at which it is generated (see Section 4, B, above). Each new level in Ex. 80 introduces or shifts a note into an unsyncopated portion of the prior time-span, with the cumulative time-span of the given pitch-class becoming syncopated at the two lower levels.

The same constraints apply to the generation of a suspension which is shorter than its resolution (see Ex. 81). Note that the

Ex. 81

prior attack of the note D, *qua* resolution, in Ex. 81b is suppressed in Ex. 81c (as indicated by the tie), as the resolution is anticipated backward into the prior time-span of the suspension.

5. The Alteration Operations

The time-span of a note may be altered by virtue of two sets of operations: 1) expansion and contraction, and 2) elision and bifurcation.

1a. Under the expansion operation, the size of a note's time-span is increased by some fraction of its original size, including fractions equal to or greater than 1.

1b. The contraction operation reduces a time-span by some fraction of the original time-span—the fraction being necessarily equal to less than 1.

2a. The elision operation superimposes a final portion of the time-span of one note on the beginning portion of a succeeding adjacent time-span of another note.

2b. The bifurcation operation effects a repetition of a time-span such that the attack-point of the repeated time-span is equivalent to that of the initial time-span with respect to metrical position. That is, under the bifurcation operation, two adjacent time-points can be equally strong (or weak) beats—an equality which is not effected by any other operation.

The alteration operations are particularly valuable at relatively background levels involving relatively large time-spans, where they produce irregularly sized phrases and sections without removing the possibility for equal-sized time-spans (bars) at foreground levels. Furthermore, these operations make it possible to alter the size of a note's time-span independent of changes in the metrical structure of surrounding time-spans. In Ex. 82b, which is expanded from Ex. 82a, the first beat of the

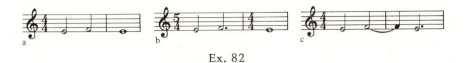

Ex. 82

second bar is the strongest beat in that bar, and is also stronger than all the beats of the preceding bar, with the exception of the first. By contrast, in Ex. 82c, which is derived from Ex. 82a, by virtue of the suspension of F, F occupies a time-span of the same size as in Ex. 82b, but with the consequence that the second E is attacked at a weaker beat and has a shorter duration than at the prior level shown in Ex. 82a. Thus, an expanded note, unlike a suspension, does not defer the attack of its linear displacement to a relatively weak beat.

Also, a note or chord can occur less than halfway between two relatively background notes without necessarily appearing to be syncopated. E.g., the third beat of Ex. 82b, bar 1, is stronger than the fourth beat—a metrical relationship which does not arise in conjunction with other operations (see Section 4, C, 1, above). Note that the fifth beat (first beat of the second bar) of Ex. 82c remains accented with respect to the fourth and sixth beats, just as in Ex. 82a, whereas in the expanded configuration of Ex. 82b, the sixth beat is stronger than the fifth beat.

Ex. 83 illustrates the expansion operation in an excerpt from the tonal literature. The first eighteen bars are divided into two phrases, eight and ten bars long, respectively. It is clear that the second phrase is modeled after the first phrase, yet the first bar of the second phrase occurs just *before* (not *at*) the halfway mark of the total eighteen-bar passage. Therefore, the problem is to circumvent a background analysis of bars 9-18 as a syncopated tonic triad anticipated from bar 10 (see Ex. 84). This is accomplished by attributing the difference in the sizes of the two phrases to the expansion of the third and fourth two-bar subsections of the first phrase into the third and fourth subsections—each of three bars—of the second phrase. In the background, each phrase is represented by a tonic triad of eight bars

Ex. 83. Mozart, *Marriage of Figaro*, Act III, "Dove sono"

Ex. 84

(Ex. 85b). Subsequently the second phrase is extended to ten bars by virtue of the above-mentioned expansions (Ex. 85c).

Ex. 85

These expansions serve to provide for motivic imitation of pitch and rhythmic configurations in preceding bars. Thus, bars 13-15 involve the filling-in of the interval G-C (bar 5), utilizing the rhythmic motive of bars 1-2 and 3-4 (a dotted quarter followed by attacks of four successive eighth-notes; see Ex. 86). With

Ex. 86

regard to bars 16-18, bar 16 includes a IV7 chord at the second beat, with the E resolving to F at the fourth eighth-note, as in bar 3; in an unexpanded version the V and I chords in bars 17-18 would presumably occur one and two beats earlier, respectively, thereby leaving no room for the pitch-rhythmic correspondence between bars 3 and 16.[4]

---

[4]   The reader will find a discussion of numerous examples of contraction and expansion in Schenker's chapter "Metrik und Rhythmik," *Der freie Satz,* pp. 183-196. Also, Hugo Riemann's *System der musikalischen Rhythmik und Metrik,* Leipzig, 1903, includes two chapters on alterations of eight-bar units, pp. 241-304.

Example 87 presents a case of elision. Bar 29 counts as a strong beat with respect to the preceding bar. However, bar 30

Ex. 87. Beethoven, Piano Sonata Op. 13, 2nd movement

counts as a strong beat with respect to bar 29—resembling the metrical accent of all the even-number bars in this phrase (bars 29-36) with respect to the preceding odd-numbered bars. (See the Appendix for further details of the metrical structure of bars 29-36 and the total movement from which Ex. 87 is excerpted.) But bar 29 can count both as the final time-point of one phrase, and the initial time-point of the *second* bar of the time-span of the following phrase. As the final time-point of the first phrase, bar 29 counts as strong; as the second bar of the following phrase, bar 29 counts as weak.

Example 88 presents a case of bifurcation. The pitch-class E, which appears only in inner parts in bars 1-3, is suspended in

Ex. 88. Chopin, Prelude Op. 28/1, bars 1-8

the soprano part in the IV7 chord in bar 5. The suspended E appears to resolve to D in the same bar, but E appears again as a suspension in bars 6 and 7. Since it strikes me as undesirable to regard the D's of bars 5-6 as lower neighbors, or to regard the E's of bars 6-7 as upper neighbors, I think of bars 5-7 as if they were just one prior bar—in a six-bar phrase—which shows up three successive times in the foreground (see Ex. 89).

Ex. 89

The reader will find other examples and explanations of the alteration operations in the Appendix.

6. Metrical Characteristics of Suspension Configurations

According to Section 4, above, a given note is generated in an unsyncopated time-span. If a predisplacement is subsequently generated as a suspension in the initial portion of the time-span of the given note, then it follows that the suspension will occupy the strongest beat in the combined time-span of suspension and resolution. Therefore, where the prior time-span of the resolution is unsyncopated, the suspension is necessarily metrically accented—i.e., occurs at a stronger beat—with respect to its resolution at the level at which the suspension is generated. (Subsequent elaborations may disguise this metrical relationship; see Chapter Five, Section 2.)

We may now consider under what conditions a suspension would be metrically unaccented with respect to its resolution (at the level at which the suspension is generated). Clearly the prior time-span of the resolution would have to be syncopated. Now, a note may occupy a syncopated time-span either due to being anticipated or suspended.

1. There would hardly seem to be any good reason for anticipating a note, only then to delay it back to its prior attack-point. See Ex. 90, where (a) and (c) are identical. On the

Ex. 90

other hand, one might anticipate a note and then delay the anticipation just partially; but in this case (Ex. 91), the suspension comes out metrically accented with respect to the attack-point of its resolution.

Ex. 91

2. A suspension can reasonably be metrically unaccented with respect to its resolution under the following conditions: a supported linear-note (the soprano D in Ex. 92a) is suspended

Ex. 92

into the time-span of its linear displacement; subsequently a predisplacement (E) of the given linear-note (D) is suspended into all of its prior time-span, thereby completely suppressing the given note in its original time-span, and converting it into an appoggiatura in the succeeding time-span. Example 92b illustrates this technique. Having encountered only one example of this sort in the tonal literature—see Ex. 162b, p. 125—I am encouraged to discount the significance of the metrically unaccented suspension in the tonal system. Henceforth I shall refer to the suspension as metrically accented with respect to its resolution, without further qualification.

The alteration operations tend to obscure the metrical levels associated with a note at the level at which it is generated. In Chapter Five, Section 1, I consider examples of metrical ambiguity arising from expansions and contractions. In these examples, suspensions are indicative of the location of metrical accents, rather than vice versa. (The last statement is based upon the presumption that other criteria besides metrical accent are sufficient for determining that a given note is in fact a suspension.)

In Chapter Five, Section 2, I discuss examples in which suspensions are unaccented with respect to their resolutions due to foreground operations introduced subsequent to the generation of the suspensions.

7. Summary

Meter involves the subordination of some beats to other beats within a given time-span. The beats at a given level relate to each other as strong and/or weak according to the hierarchy of metrical levels which pertain to a given time-span as a result of equal subdivision by a whole number n greater than 1, in connection with the application of a tonal or rhythmic operation in that time-span. The definition of syncopation is based upon relations of strong and weak beats; a syncopated time-span contains a stronger beat within it than at its inception. The metrical hierarchy at a given structural level determines the possible time-spans in which notes can be generated; according to the rule of syncopation, a note may not be newly generated in a syncopated time-span. Changes in metrical relationships among beats may be effected by the alteration operations. Finally, a suspension is normally metrically accented with respect to its resolution at the level at which the suspension is generated.

CHAPTER FOUR

COMPOSITIONAL USES OF THE SUSPENSION

Writers on tonal music have generally shown more interest in simply describing the contexts in which suspensions occur than in going on to explore the reasons for their prominence in the tonal literature. This limitation no doubt stems from the fact that many of the most important reasons for introducing suspensions concern background and middleground levels, and yet background and middleground suspensions ('large-scale suspensions') are still largely ignored in theoretical circles, despite their description and frequent illustration by Schenker in his various writings. As early as 1906, Schenker spoke of the suspension which is "prepared only mentally, i.e., . . . not explicitly set in the preceding harmony but implicitly contained therein. . . ."[1] David Beach has called attention to Schenker's description of the cadential 6/4 chord as a suspension "on the V step . . . even if the suspension lasts for a long time . . . ."[2] And although there is little outright discussion of suspensions in *Der freie Satz*, there are numerous sketches which include suspensions clearly introduced at background levels.[3]

Schenker himself spoke of the purpose of the suspension, in comparing the suspension with the accented passing-note: ". . . the suspension strives, above all, to produce the effect of a dissonance. . . ."[4] While there is indeed a strong correlation between the suspension and dissonance (see Section 1, B, below), this statement begs the ensuing question, "Why produce the effect of a dissonance?", since presumably dissonance in itself is not a self-explanatory goal. Even in recent writings by those familiar with Schenker's work, the reasons for the use of

---

[1] *Harmony*, trans. by Elizabeth Mann Borgese; ed. by Oswald Jonas, Chicago, 1954, p. 309.

[2] "The Functions of the Six-four Chord," *Journal of Music Theory*, Vol. 11/1 (1967), p. 13, and *Harmony*, p. 229.

[3] See Ex. 2, p. 15, above.

[4] *Harmony*, p. 311.

suspensions remain undisclosed. Thus, Allen Forte's textbook, *Tonal Harmony in Concept and Practice,* accounts for the suspension operation as a "process [which] creates a large and important class of dissonant harmonies,"[5] with no comment upon the significance of this fact. And David Beach describes the cadential 6/4 chord as the "product of voice-leading. . . . [Its] function is merely to delay the dominant harmony. . . ,"[6] as if the reasons for delaying a harmony were self-evident, and such delay were a matter of slight significance. While by my definition (p. 25, above) a suspension invariably delays the attack of its resolution, the effect of delay in a particular context may simply follow from the introduction of the suspension, rather than motivate it.

I put the goals of the suspension operation into three main categories.

1. Facilitation of linear displacements. There are two basic types of linear displacements in tonal music, which I shall call 'easy' and 'difficult.' The suspension is a useful way of rendering difficult displacements easy, and easy displacements still 'easier.'

2. Clarification of linear relationships in certain problematic foreground contexts, where

a) a prior linear connection would otherwise be obscured due to the foreground suppression of the predisplacement in part or all of its prior time-span;

b) an inner-part linear connection would otherwise be obscured by simultaneous activity in the outer-parts;

c) a foreground linear-note would otherwise receive overly strong harmonic support, thereby "competing" with the more background notes from which it is derived; and

d) a cadence occurring before the end of a piece would be so constructed as to evince 'total closure,' and thereby make the piece appear to end prematurely.

---

[5] New York, 1962, p. 310.
[6] *Loc. cit.*

3. Provision of contextual associations at various time-points of a piece.

    a) The suspension operation may produce harmonic associations by effecting suspension chords equivalent in pitch to chords found elsewhere in a given piece.

    b) The suspension operation can also create motivic associations by providing linear note-pairs with rhythmic features similar to those of other linear-pairs in a piece.

A given suspension may accomplish more than one goal in a given context.

1. Facilitation of Linear Displacements

A. 'Easy' and 'Difficult' Displacements

There are three types of linear displacements in tonal music: 1) displacement of an arpeggiation-note by a linear-note; 2) displacement of a linear-note by an arpeggiation-note; and 3) displacement of a linear-note by another linear-note (as in the connection of the two members of an arpeggiated diatonic fourth by the two intervening scale-degrees). The second and third types are basically alike in that the displaced note is a linear-note. So there are just two basic types of linear displacements, which are differentiated according to whether the first note is an arpeggiation-note or a linear-note.

In the first type, the predisplacement is articulated as the more background note of the linear-pair. E.g., in the linear-pair, E-D, shown in Ex. 93b, E is articulated as the background note

Ex. 93

by virtue of 1) its membership in the two outer chords of the progression, and 2) its strong harmonic support as a member of the tonic triad. With respect to harmonic support, E is actually less consonant in the I triad than D in the V triad, but as a criterion of support, membership in the tonic triad takes precedence over membership in any other triad (see p. 34, above). Indeed, the local consonance of D only partially obscures the fact that D is dissonant with respect to the tonic C of the overall context, as in Ex. 94. In summary, a linear-note is differentiated

Ex. 94

from its background predisplacement by its position between two arpeggiation-notes and/or by its relatively weak support.

The contextual stability of the background member of a linear-pair implies its prior presence throughout the total foreground time-spans of the two notes. Thus, the E of Ex. 93b occupies the time-span of D at the immediate prior level (Ex. 93a). Generally, then, in linear-pairs in which the first note is more background than the second, the sense in which the second note displaces the first is distinctly limited: for although the second note partially replaces the first note in the foreground, the context establishes this substitution as a feature of the foreground alone; in the background, the first note remains undisplaced. In addition, the background note may have a greater duration than that of the linear-note, but a linear-note rarely has a greater duration than its predisplacement at the original level of the linear-note.[7] That a note can be displaced in one sense while remaining undisplaced in another sense (in the same time-span) is the basis of Schenker's concept of levels (see Chapter Two, Section 1).

---

[7] Example 95 illustrates linear-notes which last longer than their predisplacements at the original level of generation. The arpeggiation-notes, E and A, are first anticipated and then displaced respectively by the accented passing-notes, D and G.

In the second type of linear displacement, the foreground note precedes a background note or another foreground note. The context is exactly the opposite of the context in which the first type of linear displacement occurs: here the first note is understood to occupy only its own foreground time-span and is followed eventually, if not immediately, by a contextually stable arpeggiation-note. This is illustrated in the linear connection D-C in Exx. 93b and 94.

The essential difference between the two basic types of linear displacement may be put this way: there is no "pressure" on a background predisplacement to give way to its foreground displacement; indeed, there is an outright reluctance. On the other hand, a foreground predisplacement gives way readily to a background displacement. This difference is implied by the fact that the term 'resolution' denotes the background displacement of a foreground note, and not the foreground displacement of a background note. A linear-note is relatively unstable with respect to the arpeggiation-note which it displaces, and therefore "seeks" its resolution; an arpeggiation-note is relatively stable with respect to a linear predisplacement and therefore does not seek a resolution. Of course, a single note may be an arpeggiation-note at one level and a linear-note at a prior level, e.g., the soprano D in Ex. 96. In this case, D is contextually stable with respect to the unsupported C which directly displaces it, and yet it resolves to the still more stable final soprano C.

Ex. 95

I shall call the first type of displacement 'difficult' and the second type 'easy.' In Ex. 96, the displacement of D is difficult

Ex. 96

with respect to the C enclosed in the V7 chord, and easy with respect to the soprano C in the final tonic triad. I should add that a difficult displacement is made still more difficult if the duration of the first note is substantially greater than the duration of the second note.

B. *Techniques for Easing Displacements*

There are two conditions under which the contextual weakening of the first note of a linear-pair may be desirable: 1) a displacement is difficult; and 2) a displacement is easy but the foreground linear-note is nevertheless very well supported (e.g., the D in Ex. 93b). The weakening of the first note can make a difficult displacement easy and an easy displacement still easier.

I have said (pp. 73-74, above) that two features which distinguish the background member of a linear-pair from the foreground member are positioning (as an outer or inner note of a prolongation) and harmonic support. It follows that techniques which alter positioning or change harmonic support should be effective in making displacements easier.

i) Tonicization

The standard means of altering positioning at a foreground level is tonicization. This process involves treating a subsidiary middle chord of the prolongation of a more background chord as if the middle chord itself were an outer tonic triad. This reinterpretation is achieved by interpolating certain members of the scale of the new temporary tonic (the root of the given middle chord)between the initial given tonic triad and the middle chord in question; the scale members that I have in mind are those which are chromatic with respect to the original tonic. In Ex. 97b, which is derived from Ex. 97a, the introduction of

Ex. 97

the chromatic F♯ (in conjunction with A) in a latter portion of the prior time-span of the initial I triad creates a diatonic VII/7 chord in the key of G major. The effect is to convert the soprano arpeggiation-note, E, at beat 1, into an upper neighbor-note to D, at beat 2; and to reinterpret the middle V triad as an outer tonic triad with respect to the interpolated VII/7 chord (Ex. 98). Since the bass F♯ makes E relatively dissonant with

I   VII⁷   I

Ex. 98

respect to D, the resulting displacement (E-D) is easier with respect to harmonic support as well as positioning.

Tonicizing a background V triad is a useful technique for stabilizing this chord at the end of the first part of a binary form. This is illustrated in Ex. 99. (Foreground and middleground configurations derived from this sketch are found in Exx. 104 and 105, below.)

(7̂ - 8̂)

I   V

Ex. 99

Although tonicizing is one way of easing a displacement, it has certain limitations. It works best in a context in which the given linear-note receives full triadic support (in root position), which is typical of only relatively background levels. And constant reliance on this technique would necessarily result in highly chromatic textures. There should be a means of easing displacements which exploits diatonic resources exclusively.

ii) Diatonic dissonance

Example 100 is identical to Ex. 97b in every respect except for the bass note of the second chord. This passage weakens the

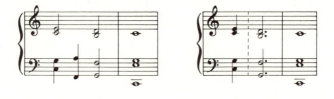

Ex. 100   Ex. 101

harmonic support of the soprano E (by virtue of the diatonic F♮) without reinterpreting E as a neighbor to D in the key of G major. The effect is problematic, however, for a diatonic dissonator tends to convert a given supported note into a foreground note which appears to be newly generated. Thus, the IV7 chord of Ex. 100 implies a background analysis in which E has a duration of just one beat, and the second beat is strong with respect to the third beat (Ex. 101), whereas in the actual background from which Ex. 100 is derived (Ex. 97a), E lasts for two beats, and the second beat is weak with respect to the third beat. One must conclude that Ex. 100 is not a suitable solution to the problem of easing the displacement of E in Ex. 97a, for it accomplishes this at the cost of distorting background relationships in the foreground.

Underling the above arguments is an analytical principle of fundamental importance: given a linear-pair in which the first member has consonant harmonic support at its initial attack-point, the presence of a dissonant reference-note in some latter portion of the time-span of the first member ordinarily implies the prior attack of the second member at the foreground attack-point of the dissonator (Exx. 100 and 101). This implication is avoided only in cases where the dissonator is clearly articulated as a note originating at a more foreground level than the supported note in question—as in Ex. 97b, where the chromatic F♯ is understood to be a foreground note just by virtue of its chromaticism. Similarly, in Ex. 102, the soprano E

Ex. 102. Beethoven, Piano Sonata Op. 14/1, Finale

is supported by B and D♯ at the second half of the second beat of bar 1 with no suggestion of a prior displacement of E at that time-point; for B and D♯ are articulated as foreground passing-notes by virtue of their temporal enclosure by the two (horizontal) note-pairs, C♯-A and E-C♯, respectively. In Ex. 103, the

Ex. 103. Beethoven, Piano Sonata Op. 13, 1st movement

harmonic support for the initial soprano C is converted (at its second attack) from an octave to the relatively dissonant major sixth. But since the new bass note, E♭, is a member of the tonic triad, and is not triadically associated with the soprano displacement, D, there is no implication of an earlier attack-point for D in the background. In Ex. 104, the headtone is G♭,

Ex. 104. Beethoven, Piano Sonata Op. 7, 3rd movement, Trio

and a G♭ is attacked as a diatonic dissonance over an inner-part A♭ in bar 12. However, the suspensions in the top part in bars 11-14 and the attack of A♮ in bar 14 articulate the soprano G♭ and F of bars 12-14 as an ornamented anticipation of the chromatically supported G♭ in bar 14. G♭ emerges as a dissonant anticipation, in bar 12, rather than as a dissonant common-tone in bar 14. The passage is analyzed in Ex. 105, and a further reduction is found above in Ex. 99.

Ex. 105

In Exx. 102-104, the diatonic dissonators are either absolutely consonant or are found in an inner part. In Ex. 100, on the other hand, F♮ is absolutely dissonant with respect to E and is in the bass part; in addition, F is approached by skip. I have found no examples in the literature of genuine weakening of a given note (predisplacement) with the features of Ex. 100, i.e., where an absolutely dissonant bass note approached by skip appears to be generated in the (prior) time-span of the given note. (A single example which might be misconstrued as such is analyzed in Chapter Five, Section 3, C, i.)

iii) The dissonant suspension

In my view of the tonal system, it is not desirable to generate a configuration *y* from a prior configuration *x,* only to deny subsequently that configuration *y* could reasonably be analytically derived from configuration *x*. Therefore, as I have indicated in the above discussion of diatonic dissonance, it is undesirable to convert a consonant note into a dissonance within its prior time-span, if that new dissonance serves as a criterion of the given note's non-presence at that prior level. But it would be entirely suitable to convert a consonant note into a dissonance *outside* its prior time-span, i.e., in a succeeding time-span. And in most cases, the extension (i.e., suspension) of a consonant note into the time-span of its displacement will result in its conversion into a dissonance, in conjunction with the other notes already present in the time-span of the displacement. For example, the bass and tenor dissonators, G, at beat 3, bar 1, Ex. 106b, are present at that beat prior to the

Ex. 106

extension of E into their time-span (Ex. 106a). Following its articulation as a well-supported triadic third, E becomes a relatively dissonant inversionally triadic sixth which proceeds easily to the triadic fifth, D. Similarly, the octave-supported alto C becomes a relatively dissonant fourth which resolves easily to the triadic third, B.

(It is presumed that the extension or delay of a note does not necessarily involve the shifting of notes originally generated in support of the shifted note. Conversely, a note would not ordinarily be articulated as a suspension where its prior harmonic support is present in a final portion of its time span; instead the given note would be regarded as a common-tone in that portion of its time span [as at the third beat of bar 1, Ex. 107]. A resolution is also typically—but not necessarily—

Ex. 107

articulated after the attack-point of its prior supporting notes. Thus, in Ex. 106b, the resolutions D and B occur after the attack of the supporting G's in the tenor and bass parts; but at the third beat of Ex. 108, neither of the notes [F and A] attacked with the suspended E and C is associated with the resolutions D and B at a prior level.)

Ex. 108

Aside from the advantage of not tampering with the background time-span of E, Ex. 106b is more suitable than Ex. 100 for another reason. In tonal music, some rhythmic configurations are more regular or basic than others. The prototype of rhythmic regularity is the articulation of notes in equally bisected portions of a prior time-span. The further away from equal bisection, the more irregular is the resultant rhythmic configuration. In Ex. 106b, D occurs at the fourth beat of a prior time-span of E, suggesting the possibility that at a prior level D may have occurred at the metrically stronger third beat—which in turn suggests that E intrudes upon the time-span of D in the foreground. In Ex. 100, on the other hand, D bisects the prior time-span of E, and therefore occurs at the most regular available time-point; so E is articulated exclusively in a rhythmically stable context (beats 1 and 2). The rhythmic context of Ex. 106b supports the harmonic context in articulating E at the third beat as an unstable note in the prior time-span of D. (Of course, it is feasible for a linear-note to be originally generated in the final fourth of the prior time-span of a preceding arpeggiation-note, as in the case of D in Ex. 107. But in this case, *all* the notes generated in support of E at beat 1 are also present at beat 3, and the notes supporting D are present [with the exception of the tenor G] only in the time-span of D. In Ex. 106b, E no longer has root-position support at the third beat, and two of the notes supporting D [the tenor and bass G's] are attacked at a stronger beat than D itself.)

iv) The consonant suspension

The two principal factors in the facilitation of a linear displacement by diatonic means are harmonic weakening and rhythmic irregularity—two aspects of tonal music which are associated primarily with the foreground. Harmonic weakening usually involves rhythmic irregularity, as in a suspension configuration, where the suspension and the resolution may be attacked independently of the notes with which they were originally associated. But rhythmic irregularity does not necessarily involve harmonic weakening; a suspension may be attacked independently of the notes originally associated with it and yet become relatively consonant. This requires some justification, for what is the point of weakening a note in its rhythmic context while strengthening it in its harmonic context?

A consonant suspension suggests that other reasons are to be found for the suspension instead of or besides facilitating displacements. In many cases, the first note of a linear-pair is displaced so easily, for reasons independent of harmonic support, that no amount of added harmonic support will obfuscate the basic ease of the displacement. For example, in Ex. 109, the soprano linear-note, D, is harmonically strength-

Ex. 109. Mozart, *Marriage of Figaro*, Act I, "Non so più"

ened by virtue of being suspended, but its displacement (by E♭) remains easy because of the clear articulation of D as a non-member of the tonic triad. The reason for introducing the suspension is to imitate the dissonant suspended B♮ in the preceding bar (see Section 3, B, below). (The increased length of the second suspension and the consequent emphasis on delay are associated with Cherubino's desire to linger in the amatory atmosphere of the Countess' bedroom; the G minor triad resulting from the suspension relates also to the music accompanying the Count's arrival in the ensuing recitative.)

If a consonant suspension occurs in the immediate vicinity of one or more dissonant suspensions, the consonant suspension is likely to seem dissonant as well. This effect is illustrated in Ex. 110, where the consonant alto suspensions E♮ and G♮, in

Ex. 110. Chopin, Étude Op. 10/6, bars 33-36

bar 2, occur concurrently with the dissonant soprano suspension, B♭. Another example is found in Ex. 111, where the

Ex. 111. Beethoven, Piano Sonata Op. 2/3, 1st movement, bars 69-73

suspended consonant left-hand D in bar 4 comes immediately after and before the dissonant bass suspensions, E and C, respectively. I regard D as a suspension in spite of its consonance (and the fact that the linear-pair D-C represents a difficult displacement), because of the overall series of dissonant suspensions in the left-hand part; to regard D (in the bass part) as a common-tone at the second beat of bar 4 would be to ignore the consistent eighth-note delay throughout all four bars.

C. *Other Aspects of the Easing of Displacements*

i) Chromatic reference-notes

Although diatonic dissonance in connection with a suspension is a suitable means of making a linear displacement easier, no objection can be made to a suspension which is dissonant due to a chromatic reference-note (such as F♯ at beat 3, Ex. 103). Typically, when a chromatic dissonator is introduced into the *original* time-span of the background predisplacement, the latter is suspended over a diatonic dissonator as well. This technique is illustrated in Ex. 112. Diatonic and chromatic dissonators may also be found in successive portions of the time-span of a suspension (Ex. 113c).

Ex. 112. Brahms, Symphony No. 3, 2nd movement

ii) Triadic harmonic support for suspensions

Just as a passing-note can be given triadic support (see the soprano D in Ex. 106a) without obscuring its position as a relatively foreground note at that level, a suspension can be given triadic support without spoiling the ease of the displace-

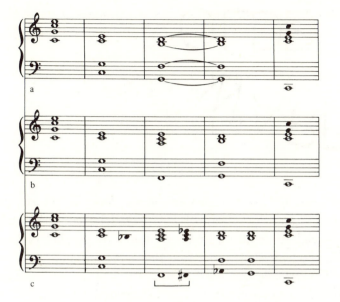

Ex. 113. Background sketch, Bach, *Well-Tempered Clavier*, Vol. 1, Prelude 1. [See pp. 119-122 for justification of the analysis of E and C in the IV7 chord of this example as suspensions.]

ment which the suspension is meant to effect. In Ex. 114, the suspended alto C is given triadic support as the fifth of an F major triad. This fifth support is weaker than the octave

Ex. 114

support for C at the first beat, but remains stronger than the support for the resolution, B, as the third of the G major triad. Since the rhythmic pattern in the soprano part is more regular than in the alto part, the B and supporting G's appear to be delayed, instead of the D appearing to be anticipated. (See the discussion of rhythmic regularity, p. 83, above.)

Unlike Ex. 114, no members of the original V triad remain at the third beat of Ex. 115; therefore, the alto C might in this

Ex. 115

case be regarded as a consonant common-tone (at the third beat). But C and the soprano E have parallel origins as members of the initial tonic triad, and two notes of parallel origin are generally considered to occupy the same original time-span. Since the metrically accented dissonance of E (at the third beat) articulates it as a suspension, C is articulated as a suspension as well. (See the discussion of consonant suspensions, p. 85, above.) Another factor in Ex. 115 is that the notes which support the suspended alto C (F and A) are metrically accented linear-notes; C is correspondingly articulated as a quasi-linear-note in their time-span.

Example 116 offers still another instance of a triadically supported suspension—the alto A of the IV6/5 chord in bar 2.

Ex. 116. Bach, *St. Matthew Passion,* Chorale: "Wer hat dich so geschlagen."

My contention that in these three examples the bass note of the suspension chord is generated as triadic support for the suspension is based on the fact that while suspensions abound in 6-5-3 and 7-5-3 chords (Exx. 114 and 115, respectively), they never occur in chords built on $\hat{4}$ which do not contain a perfect fifth above the bass. The parenthetical chords in Ex. 117 are unlikely, because they contain no suspensions the support of

Ex. 117

which justifies the generation of the bass note, F. Even with a suspended C (Ex. 118), the presence of F in the bass is rare when A is not also present in another part to complete the IV

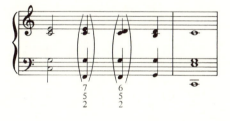

Ex. 118

triad. Example 119 illustrates an exceptional case of a 7-5-2 suspension chord (the "5"—G—being implied from the preceding chord).

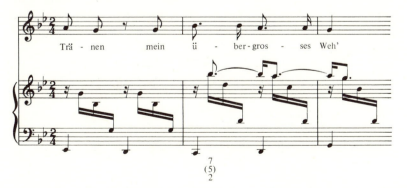

Ex. 119. Schumann, *Dichterliebe,* "Hör ich das Liedchen klingen," bars 18-20

The traditional numerical labels assigned to suspension configurations—usually determined by the respective intervals formed by the suspension and resolution with a common reference-note—are inappropriate for triadically supported suspensions. In Ex. 116, the suspended alto A of bar 2 forms a perfect fifth with the bass reference-note D, while the resolution G forms a third with the bass note E. To label the suspension pair "5-3" would misleadingly imply a non-linear resolution.

A semblance of consonant support for suspensions is found in examples where the suspension is dissonant with respect to an inner part, but consonant with respect to the bass. Since outer parts generally take precedence over inner parts in tonal music the suspension appears well supported; at the same time, the inner-part dissonance facilitates the displacement. In Ex. 120a, which enharmonically clarifies the diatonic relationships

Ex. 120. Wagner, *Die Walküre,* Act III, Finale

of Ex. 120b, the suspended soprano A ♯ is consonant compared to A ♮, with respect to the bass D♯, but is dissonant with respect to the tenor C♮. In Ex. 121, the suspended soprano E

Ex. 121. Beethoven, Piano Sonata Op. 10/3, 2nd movement

in bar 2 is consonant compared to F, with respect to the bass
G♯, but dissonant with respect to the alto D.

  iii) The suspension of harmonically well-supported linear-
       notes

An interesting side effect of the suspending of a well-
supported linear-note is that in the course of making an easy
displacement still easier, the linear-note *qua* suspension is
presented literally in the weak harmonic context which its
supporting notes seek to obviate. In Ex. 122a, D and B♮ in bar
2 are attacked jointly with C and E♭, although the tenor and

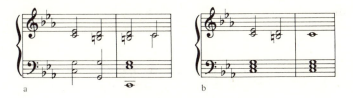

Ex. 122

bass G's in bar 1 are generated as consonant support for D and
B♮—in order to avoid their being articulated as dissonances
against the C and E♭ of the prior tonic triad in that bar (Ex.
122b). The well-supported linear-note, B♮, is presented in this
fashion in the last bar of Ex. 123.

Ex. 123. Bach, *St. Matthew Passion*, Finale

  iv) Background predisplacements of long duration

In a passage where a displacement is difficult because of the
relatively long duration as well as strong harmonic support of
the first member of a linear-pair, a suspension is a virtual

necessity in bringing about the displacement. In Ex. 124, the background soprano C♯ of bar 1 is suspended and displaced by

Ex. 124. Schubert, *Winterreise*, "Die Nebensonnen"

the sixteenth-note B in bar 3. Example 125 presents the same passage with the C♯ in bar 3 articulated as a common-tone[8] —due to the reattack of I in place of V at that time-point. The

Ex. 125

suspension of C♯ in Ex. 124 assists the difficult motion to B, whereas the absence of the suspension in Ex. 125 makes the cadence seem ineffective and premature; the B, in contrast to the weighty C♯ supported in the I triad, is too unsubstantial to represent the displacement of the background C♯, and instead sounds like a passing-note, local to bar 4. Although Schubert varied the harmonization of this melodic line throughout the song, he invariably weakened the harmonic support for C♯ before displacing it with B at a cadence.

Another example of this type is found in Ex. 126; the background $\hat{3}$ originating in bar 1 is articulated as the preparation [of a suspension] in the voice part of bar 7, and is heard as a suspension in the first violin part of bar 8.

---

[8] The difference between a suspension and a common-tone is discussed in Chapter Five, Section 3, C.

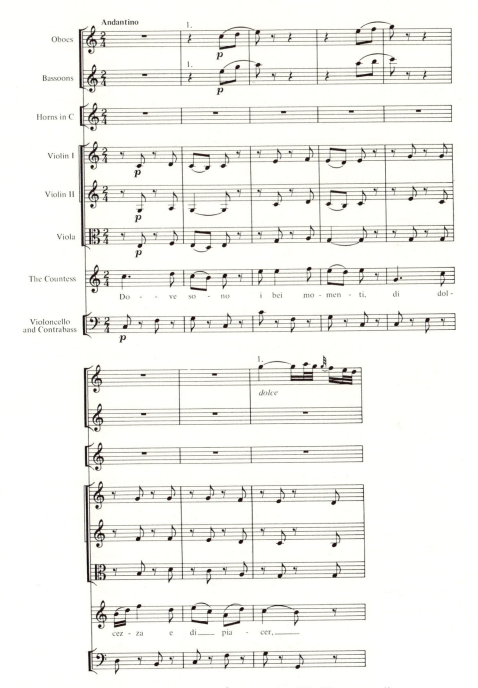

Ex. 126. Mozart, *Marriage of Figaro*, Act III, "Dove sono"

Example 127 is a counter-example, since the background $\hat{3}$ is reattacked, but not as a suspension, in bar 7 before its

Ex. 127. Beethoven, Piano Sonata Op. 2/3, Scherzo

displacement in bar 8. Notice, however, that in this case, the reattack of $\hat{3}$/I occurs as a weak upbeat relative to the cadential beat at which $\hat{2}$ is attacked.

v) Resolution doublings

There is a familiar compositional rule that a suspension should not be supported with the simultaneous articulation of an instance of the pitch-class of its resolution. Since generally a block chord would be generated prior to the delay of one of its members (see the final I chord of Ex. 123), the rule should more properly read: "A suspension should not be generated in a time-span already occupied in another voice by a member of the same pitch-class as its resolution."

There is some justification for this rule, insofar as the delay of the resolution is an integral feature of suspension configurations. The simultaneous attack of a suspension with an instance of the pitch-class of its resolution (i.e., a resolution doubling) might have the effect of countermanding the sense of delay effected by the suspension. However, resolution doublings are quite common, particularly octave, as opposed to unison, doublings (see the soprano D in bar 2 of Ex. 128, as well as the

Ex. 128. Bach, *Well-Tempered Clavier*, Vol. 1, Prelude 8

final bass C in Ex. 123). A unison resolution doubling is more likely to spoil the delay effect of a suspension, especially where the displacement is by half-step (Ex. 129); but it is not a serious problem in the case of a whole-step displacement (D-C, tenor part, Ex. 130, bar 2).

Ex. 129

Ex. 130. Bach, Cantata No. 13, Chorale:
"So sei nun Seele, deine," bars 6-8

2. Clarification of Linear Relationships

A. *Foreground Emphasis on Prior Linear Connections*

i) Supression of the first note of a linear-pair in the latter part of its prior time-span

In Ex. 131a, the headtone, E♮, occupies the first six bars of an eight-bar passage. Subsequent operations leading to Exx.

Exx. 131a and b

Ex. 131c

Ex. 131d. Beethoven, Piano Sonata Op. 13, Finale

131c and d involve the suppression of the soprano E♭ in the final half (bars 4-6) of its prior time-span. This results in a significant gap between the discontinuation of E♭ and the attack of its background registral displacement, D, in bar 7. But the prior suspension of E♭ (Ex. 131b) assures the retention of the original temporal and registral adjacency of E♭ –D at a relatively foreground level. (In the immediate foreground, the upper neighbor, F, intervenes between E♭ and D in bar 7; the temporal adjacency of E♭ –D remains transparent nonetheless, due to the lack of rhythmic and harmonic support for F.)

Introducing a suspension is not the only means of retaining foreground temporal adjacency between the notes of a linear-pair; the first note can be reattacked as a common-tone. But as I indicated above, in the discussion of long-held background predisplacements (see pp. 91-92, above) the attack of a background displacement may appear to be premature and ineffective unless its predisplacement is weakened by some means. For this reason, the metrically strong reattack of the headtone as a common-tone (with tonic support) just before the attack of its background displacement would rarely work well as a means of retaining temporal adjacency in the foreground (cf. Exx. 124-125).

Another instance of retained adjacency is found in Ex. 132, where the initial soprano F in bar 1 is displaced by E in bar 3

Ex. 132. Beethoven, Piano Sonata Op. 10/3, 2nd movement

after a more foreground upper-neighbor displacement by G in bar 2. Without the prior suspension of F in bar 3, the connection between F and E would be obscured in the foreground. I should add that Ex. 132 differs from Ex. 131 in one significant respect: although in Ex. 131 the soprano E♭ of bar 6 is suppressed, E♭ is nonetheless present as a pitch in a lower register, so that only the background *registral* adjacency of E♭ –D is at stake; in Ex. 132, bar 2, the pitch-class F is suppressed in *all* registers.

ii) Suppression of the first note of a linear-pair in all but the latter part of its prior time-span

The purpose of the suspension operation in this classification is to give added weight—literally, duration—to the first note of a linear-pair to counter its subsequent deemphasis, due to suppression in most of its prior time-span. In Ex. 133, the initial

Ex. 133

soprano G♯ occupies the entire first bar; in Ex. 134, the
soprano G♯ is suppressed in all but the final twelfth of the first
bar (in the voice part). The suspension of G♯ in bar 2 extends
the note by one-third of its prior duration—thereby giving it

Ex. 134. Schumann, *Liederkreis* Op. 39, "Waldesgespräch"

foreground prominence despite its virtually complete suppression in the soprano part of the preceding bar. It is worth noting
that on the occasion of the reprinting of the *Liederkreis* Op. 39
by a new publisher, Schumann made numerous changes in the
original score,[9] among them the addition to "Waldesgespräch"
of the suspended G♯ (Ex. 134) and several other suspensions,
each serving to extend a partially suppressed preparation.

Another example of the same kind is found in Ex. 135,
where the soprano eighth-note A♭ of bar 1 is suspended into
bar 2. At a prior level the soprano A♭ occupies the entire first
bar. In both of these examples, the suspension facilitates a
difficult linear displacement.

[8] See Leopold Hirschberg, "Merkwürdiges aus einem Schumann-Erst-
druck," *Die Musik,* Vol. 21/10 (1929), pp. 731-736.

Ex. 135. Beethoven, Piano Sonata Op. 7, 2nd movement, bars 25-27

iii) Total registral suppression in a prior time-span

The tonic (C major) triad occupies the first two-thirds of the time-span of Ex. 136a. One of the potential linear connections of the configuration is E-D, but note that the soprano D in the

Ex. 136. Background sketch, Chopin, Prelude Op. 28/1, bars 1-8 [cf. Ex. 88, p. 66, above]

last third of the total time-span is not preceded by the pitch E in the same (high) register. Subsequently, the pitch-class E of the I triad is suspended in the higher soprano register (Ex. 136b), with the consequence that the potential contextual connection between E and D is realized in the actual foreground. (Cf. Ex. 88, p. 66 for the latter and for further discussion of this passage. An analysis of the complete piece is found in Felix Salzer's *Structural Hearing*.) [10]

iv) Total pitch-class suppression in a prior time-span

Bars 1-5 of Ex. 137 represent a foreground passage in which the tonic E♭ is present in inner parts, but the other two

[10]   New York, 1952, 1962, Ex. 492, Vol. 2, p. 279.

Ex. 137. Beethoven, Piano Sonata Op. 31/3, 1st movement

members of the tonic triad, G and B♭, are totally suppressed in those bars. In bar 6, G finally appears as a suspension, along with E♭, over B♭. Then E♭ resolves to D at the downbeat of bar 7, and G resolves to F a half-beat later. The soprano F of bars 1-3 functions as an incomplete lower neighbor which connects to its displacement, the suspended G, via the passing G♭ of bars 4-5.

Another illustration of a totally suppressed preparation is found at the beginning of Brahms' Second Symphony. The F♯ of the explicit I6/4 chord in bars 2-3 is prepared as a member of the tonic triad implied in bar 1 by the single bass motion, D-C♯-D.

B. *Relative Obscurity of an Inner-Part Linear Connection*

In tonal music, inner-part connections tend to be overshadowed by outer-part events. For example, in Ex. 138a, the

Ex. 138

alto connection C-B is relatively obscure in comparison to the outer-part motions, E-D and C-G. In Ex. 138b, this "contextual neglect" is rectified; the C-B connection is now articulated at a time-point at which no other note is attacked.

Other examples where a suspension isolates and emphasizes
a linear connection are found in Ex. 139, where in bars 1-5 a

Ex. 139. Mozart, String Quartet K. 465, 2nd movement

note in the top part of each bar is displaced by a note in an
inner part of the succeeding bar; and in Ex. 140a, where the
alto F is displaced by E♮ in the soprano (see Ex. 140b, bar 8).

Ex. 140a.

Ex. 140b. Beethoven, Piano Sonata Op. 2/1, 1st movement

Each of these examples involves contexts in which stepwise displacements would be articulated—albeit not as emphatically —even in the absence of the suspensions. In some cases, a suspension actually creates a displacement between adjacent notes, in that the displacement exists only by virtue of the suspension. Normally, where a given outer-part note moves to another note a half-step away in the same part, another note a whole-step away in the opposite direction is not also viewed as its displacement unless no alternative analysis is available. Thus, in Ex. 141a, the inner-part B♭ is articulated as a displacement

Ex. 141

of the top-part C only because B♭ is neither a common-tone from the preceding chord nor a displacement of a note in another part. On the other hand, the B♭ of Ex. 141b is articulated solely as a displacement of A♭, since the parallelism of the alto and soprano motions emphasizes the A♭–B♭ connection to the exclusion of the latent C–B♭ connection. Example 141c shows the exploitation of this latent connection: the suspension of C with the simultaneous attack of the undelayed D♭ converts B♭ into a resolution of C occurring independently of the C–D♭ connection. This motion is present in bars 5-6 of Ex. 139.

An optional method for isolating a linear connection from other tonal events is to anticipate the displacement. This arrangement is generally not so satisfactory as the suspending of the predisplacement; instead of facilitating a displacement, it works to the opposite effect by weakening the harmonic support for the second note of the displacement pair. Thus, in the alto line of bar 1, Ex. 142b, the displacement B is a dis-

Ex. 142

sonant seventh at the second beat; at a prior level B appears only as a consonance (at the third and fourth beats, Ex. 142a).

C. *Excessive Harmonic Support for a Linear-Note (Parallel Octaves and Fifths)*

In Ex. 143, a neighbor motion, E♭-D♮-E♭, is found in the bass part, thereby providing octave support for the soprano D♮ in bar 3. Octave support of this kind would ordinarily be

Ex. 143. Bach, *Well-Tempered Clavier*, Vol. 1, Prelude 8

undesirably strong for a linear-note. In this case, however, the bass E♭ is suspended in bar 3, thereby delaying the attack of the lower D♮ and considerably weakening the foreground harmonic support for the upper D♮. Of course, the two octave equivalents are still present during a joint time-span (the upper D♮ is implied by virtue of being undisplaced at beats 2 and 3 of bar 3), but their attack-points no longer coincide. And the E♭-D♮ connection is facilitated in the bass part by the substitution of a major seventh for the octave at the attack-point of the soprano D♮.

The simultaneous attack of two octave equivalents could be obviated by suspending the upper E♭, rather than the lower one, but with less satisfactory results. In both cases, the total duration of the joint articulation of the octave displacements is reduced; but in the case of the soprano suspension, its resolution (D♮) is strongly supported (consonant) at its attack-point (Ex. 144a), while with the bass suspension it is not (Ex. 144b).

Ex. 144

Another solution to the problem of excessive support for a linear-note would be to delay the attack of the supporting note merely through supression, without the suspension of its predisplacement (Ex. 145). Comparison of Exx. 143 and 145

Ex. 145

indicates that the soprano-bass interval at the attack-point of the upper D♮ is much more dissonant with the suspension of E♭ than without it (E♭-D vs. F-D).

Without the delay of the bass D♮ in bar 3, Ex. 143 would contain implied parallel octaves from bar 2 to bar 3. I do not wish to take up in detail the merits or faults of parallel fifths and octaves, as the issue is a complicated one which would require fuller treatment than there is room for here. Certainly there is no obvious solution which renders all parallel fifths and octaves equally good or bad; but to the extent that they are to be avoided in the foreground, the suspension provides one way out, as in Ex. 143.

I wish to point out in this connection that a linear-note ordinarily does not receive the same type or degree of harmonic support as the arpeggiation-notes which enclose it. Since the strongest harmonic support is provided by the octave and perfect fifth (see the discussion of consonance and dissonance, pp. 28-30, above), a general prohibition of parallel octaves and fifths can be understood in this light. However, as we have seen in Ex. 143, the undesirable effect of strong parallel harmonic support can be offset by suspending the bass note which supports the first member of a linear-pair.[11]

In a famous passage involving both parallel fifths and a suspension, the suspension occurs in one of the parts *not* involved in the fifths (Ex. 146a), bars 222-223). The notation of the second bassoon part is the cause for some confusion here, since the motion D♯-D♮ over A♭-G (in the bass and cello) does not literally exemplify parallel fifths. However, the D♯, which is appropriate for the B major chord in bar 216, should properly be renotated in bar 222 as E♭, a member of the German-sixth chord used to retonicize C.

---

[11] Fux gives a similar example involving parallel fifths which are made acceptable due to suspensions of successive bass notes. See *Gradus ad Parnassum,* Figs. 137-138, p. 95.

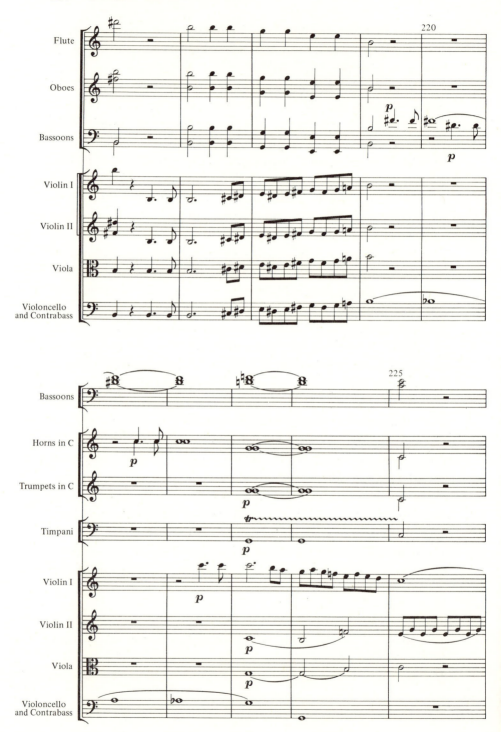

Ex. 146a. Mozart, Symphony K. 551, Finale, bars 216-225

The fifths are justified here, according to the following reasoning: the effect of a tonicization is to reinterpret a linear-note arising in a relatively background configuration as an arpeggiation-note in a relatively foreground configuration (see the discussion of tonicization, pp. 76-78, above). In bars 223-224, D is a linear-note in a background prolongation of a C triad, but is an arpeggiation-note at the subsequent level at which E♭ and F♯ (in the preceding bar) tonicize G. From the viewpoint of a G tonic, the fifth support for E♭ (as a linear-note relating to D) is too strong, since it is equal to the fifth support for D (Ex. 146b). But the bass A♭ emphasizes C as a tonic

5 - 5

Ex. 146b

(since in the tonal system there is no G scale with A♭ as second degree, whereas A♭ is the sixth degree of C minor), and from this viewpoint it is the fifth support for D which is too strong—E♭ being associated now with C as tonic (Ex. 146c).

5 - 5

Ex. 146c

The parallel fifths are justified insofar as they serve to clarify the dual structural function of the G triad (as V and I) as well as of the soprano D (as linear-note and arpeggiation-note) in this passage. Since the pitch relationships in this passage emphasize neither E♭ nor D as an outright foreground note with respect to the other, there is therefore no outright case of overly strong support for either of the notes. This explains why no suspension is needed to cancel the parallel fifths.[1][2]

[12] It might be argued that my defense of the parallel fifths in Ex. 146a is invalidated by the fact that passages of this sort are rarely found in the literature. It is quite true that a German-sixth chord is typically followed by a cadential I6/4, not a V5/3, thereby avoiding parallel fifths. But the 6/4 chord is generally a double-suspension chord, and one can usually find more positive reasons for the presence of the suspensions (as in several categories described in this chapter) than the mere avoidance of fifths. In the eighth bar of the theme of the last movement of Beethoven's Piano Sonata Op. 109, Beethoven seems to have carefully avoided explicit fifths by omitting F♯ from the dominant cadence (see Ex. 147)—an omission

Ex. 147. Beethoven, Piano Sonata Op. 109, Finale

which is found consistently in the variations as well, in the absence of a 6/4 chord. But I do not take this omission very seriously since in any case one regards the G♮ as being displaced by F♯ at the attack-point of the B triad (V). In the classical period there was, as now, a widespread belief in the unsuitability of parallel fifths; therefore I feel that Beethoven's practice here may be interpreted as "playing the game." (In the same way, one can understand Mozart's retention of the notated D♯ throughout Ex. 146a. And it can be presumed that some people would be fully convinced, by the notation, that parallel fifths were indeed avoided in this passage; for I have encountered a description of a "doubly augmented fourth chord" [A♭-C-D♯-F♯] as a special category of augmented sixth chord. See R. F. Goldman, *Harmony in Western Music,* 1965, p. 88.) Certainly this would not be the first example of notational manipulations to avoid the appearance of parallel fifths: a generally highly admired practice of ancient vintage has been to disguise parallel fifths by means of voice exchanges under the dubious assumption that change in vocal or instrumental timbre is invariably sufficient to counter structural "flaws."

D. *Avoidance of Premature Total Closure*

If the term 'closure' is understood as 'symptom of finality,' then one can say that a time-point which evinces total closure is the structural ending of a piece. (The concept of 'coda' arises from the notion that a structural ending may itself be prolonged, so that the structural ending and the actual ending of a piece need not coincide.) Just as it is often useful to employ some aspects of closure at the end of a principal section of a large piece or movement, it is correspondingly essential to *avoid* total closure before a structural ending. Example 148 is

Ex. 148

an unsuitable middleground prolongation, because the first three chords comprise a "complete piece"; and the continuation appears to be the start of another passage, or is at the very least ambiguous in its relation to the preceding three chords. The most prominent aspects of total closure are the melodic scale degrees $\hat{2}$-$\hat{1}$ supported in a block chord V-I progression. A suitable technique for avoiding total closure is to arrange the attack-points of the bass and soprano notes in such a way that $\hat{2}$ and $\hat{1}$ are not attacked at the same time-points as V and I, respectively.

The end of the first phrase of the slow movement of Beethoven's Piano Sonata Op. 7 (Ex. 149b) is announced by the

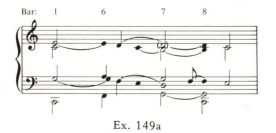

Ex. 149a

Ex. 149b. Beethoven, Piano Sonata Op. 7, 2nd movement

V-I cadence in bars 7-8. The sense of total closure which would follow from the simultaneous attack of $\hat{2}$/V and $\hat{1}$/I, respectively, is avoided here through the suppression of $\hat{2}$ in its original time-span (bar 7) and the delay of $\hat{1}$ (bar 8—see Ex. 149a). Since only triadic intervals are associated with genuine total closure, the attack of members of the V triad in bar 8 effect non-triadic intervals at the prior attack-point of the concluding I triad.

The same technique can be used at the end of a movement. However, I would not ordinarily expect to find this technique used both within and at the end of a movement without some differentiation between the two endings. In the slow movement of Beethoven's Piano Sonata Op. 2/1, one finds delayed melodic closure both in bar 8 (Ex. 150a) and also at the next to

Ex. 150. Beethoven, Piano Sonata Op. 2/1, 2nd movement

Ex. 150 (cont.)

last bar of the movement (bar 60, Ex. 150b). Bar 60 does not represent the structural ending of the movement, however; this is found in bar 58 (Ex. 150c). Example 150b contains a coda which prolongs the structurally important tonic triad of bar 58 (Ex. 150c). (I do not regard the final V-I motion in Bar 61 as the structural ending because of the long preceding rest, the soft dynamics, and the staccato articulation; the effect is too much that of an afterthought.)

3. Contextual Associations

A. *Harmonic Associations*

In any sequence of dissonant suspensions, each suspension chord is necessarily associated with all the others just by virtue of the series of dissonant intervals formed in connection with the suspensions. Example 139 (p. 101) exhibits a succession of suspension chords producing this kind of harmonic association. A suspension chord can also be associated with a dissonant chord which originates other than as a suspension chord. In Ex. 140b (p. 102), the background G of the V chord is anticipated in the soprano register in bar 7 and is attacked in the tenor part during its original time-span, bar 8. A new chord—the II6/5 in bar 7—is generated in support of the anticipated G: the bass B♭ forms a consonant interval with G (a major sixth), in contrast to the dissonant interval formed between G and the prior bass note of that time-span, F (a major ninth). In addition, the background alto F—a tonic pitch which remains well supported as a member of the B♭ minor triad that is included within the II6/5 chord—is suspended in the soprano part in bar 8. The harmonic association comes at the end of the movement (see Ex. 151).

Ex. 151. Beethoven, Piano Sonata Op. 2/1, 1st movement

Here the top-line configuration of bars 7-8 (Ex. 140b) is repeated within the top-line configurations of bars 146-152, with F again suspended in the top part (bar 151). On this occasion, there is no anticipation of G; but the II 6/5 chord is present all the same—as the suspension chord in bar 151.

B. *Motivic Associations*

A suspension can provide a motivic imitation of a linear displacement achieved by a tonal or rhythmic operation. In Ex. 135 (p. 99), the suspension of the soprano A♭ in bar 2 is followed by the suspension of the soprano A♮ in bar 3. The purpose of suspending A♭ is to give it added duration, since it is registrally suppressed throughout most of its prior time-span as preparation (bar 1). The suspension of A♮ cannot be similarly justified nor be explained by any of the other goals of suspensions listed previously in this chapter: the A♮ is in an outer part, its displacement by B♭ is easy, and it occupies its entire original time-span *qua* preparation (the third beat of bar 2). The purpose of suspending A♮ is to provide an immediate motivic imitation of the suspended A♭ in the preceding bar.

In Ex. 152, the tenor passing-note A♭ after beat 2 of bar 1 is imitated by eighth-note linear-pairs in three of the four

Ex. 152. Bach, Cantata No. 159, Chorale: "Jesu, deine Passion"

succeeding beats, as well as later in the piece. The first two of these pairs (D-C and C-B♭) are suspension pairs. (See p. 146 below, re the third pair, E♭-D♭.)

The second movement of Beethoven's Moonlight Sonata employs a suspension motive throughout bars 9-16, as a varied repetition of bars 1-8. (This example is quoted by Allen Forte in *Tonal Harmony in Concept and Practice*,[13] and is quoted below as Ex. 171 in the discussion of suppressed resolutions, pp. 132-133).

At the first beat of bar 3, Ex. 124 (p. 92), the soprano suspension pair, C♯-B, imitates the rhythmic-pitch pattern arising from the sixteenth-note anticipations, B and C♯, introduced in the first two bars, respectively. A complementary goal is to establish a suspension motive which is subsequently imitated as a result of some operation other than the suspension operation. In Ex. 134 (p. 98), the suspension of G♯ in bar 2 is imitated by the anticipated accented neighbor, C♯, in the next bar.

I have had occasion to refer to motivic imitation in the discussion of consonant suspensions, pp. 84-86.

We have seen in this chapter that the suspension can serve a variety of compositional functions. In the foreground, the suspension operation can effect contextual similarities, as well as clarify note relationships arising at prior levels. And in the background—indeed, at all levels—the suspension can add to the sense of flow by undermining the stability of prior notes as they are displaced in linear configurations.

[13] Pages 311-312.

CHAPTER FIVE

THE ANALYSIS OF SUSPENSIONS

A suspension configuration has certain metrical and pitch relationships at the level at which the suspension originates. These characteristics are not unique to suspension configurations, nor are they immutable at subsequent levels. Section 1 takes up examples of suspension configurations in which there is some ambiguity as to where the principal metrical accents occur. Section 2 illustrates some of the types of foreground configurations in which suspensions occur. Section 3 deals with the criteria by which suspension configurations can be differentiated from similar configurations effected by other tonal and rhythmic operations.

1. Suspensions and Metrical Accent

Suspensions are normally metrically accented at the level at which they are generated (see Chapter Three, Section 6). Therefore, metrical accent is an analytical criterion of suspensions: the presence of a predisplacement at a relatively strong beat with respect to the attack-point of its displacement adds to any other criteria which may suggest that the predisplacement is suspended. However, a suspension may be shifted in the foreground to a relatively weak beat with respect to the attack-point of its resolution (see Section 2,A, below). So one cannot presume that a note is not a suspension just because it is located at a relatively weak beat in the foreground. Moreover, the typical four-square metrical notation of tonal music often makes a given note *look* metrically weak even though it does not sound so; metrical notation cannot be trusted to invariably reflect essential structural relationships.[1] And finally, in various

---

[1] On the relationship between real and notated meter, Edward T. Cone has recently written the following: "Normally, to be sure, the two coincide, but there are frequent exceptions. The extension or the elision of a cadence occasionally shifts a passage (even a thematic return) to the "wrong" half of a 4/4 measure. In most of these cases the true measure

types of middleground configurations, the presence of a suspension may itself be a guide to the location of a strong metrical accent, rather than vice versa. Clearly other suspension criteria must be relatively forthright if metrical accents are to be determined by the presence of suspensions. I shall present here some examples in which suspensions clarify misleading foreground metrical notation, and determine the location of large-scale metrical accents.

A. *Suspensions at Apparently Weak Beats*

The division of a time-span by n, where n is the final member of more than one sequence of multiples (see Chapter Three, Sections 3 and 4, A) can lead to metrical ambiguity. A common situation involves equal subdivision where $n = 6$, leading to confusion as to whether the result is two groups of three or three groups of two—the so-called hemiola effect. A similar effect is produced when two adjacent time-spans of equal size are divided into six beats each—one time-span as two groups of three beats, the other as three groups of two beats. We find an instance of this kind of metrical ambiguity in Ex. 153a: bars 39-41 are appropriately notated in 3/4 meter,

Ex. 153a. Mozart, *Requiem,* "Hostias"

itself has been shifted, the composer not having felt it necessary (or conventionally allowable) to change the metric notation. Such shifts explain a number of puzzling passages that today would be clarified by notating a temporary change of meter." See *Musical Form and Musical Performance,* New York, 1968, pp. 72-73.

whereas bars 42-43 comprise six beats more accurately notated as one large 3/2 bar (with the exception of the tenor part, Ex. 153b). Observe that the soprano E♮ at beat 2 of bar 43 (Ex.

Ex. 153b

153a) is a suspension which occurs at an apparently weak beat with respect to the attack-point of its resolution D at beat 3. (See Chapter Three, Section 3 p. 54, above, re the metrical relationship between the second and third beats in triple meter.) But as Ex. 153b shows, the suspended E♮ is actually located at the first beat of a two-beat time-span and is metrically accented with respect to its resolution.

In sarabandes, where notes commonly occupy both the second and third beats of a 3/4 bar, it is often profitable to consider each bar as basically duple, with the second beat expanded (see Chapter Three, Section 5) into two beats in the foreground. In Exx. 154c and 155c one finds suspensions

Ex. 154. Bach, French Suite in E, Sarabande, bars 15-16

attacked at a second beat and resolved at the following relatively strong third beat. In these contexts one regards the third beat as the second half of a prior second beat (see Exx.

Ex. 155. Bach, French Suite in E, Sarabande, bars 23-24

154 a and b and 155 a and b). But hemiola is not effected, since here, unlike in Ex. 153, the second beat of *every* bar is emphasized.

In Ex. 149b (p. 110), the soprano C of bar 4 is a suspension attacked at the second beat and resolved at the (apparently) stronger third beat. (I provide a justification for my analysis of C as a suspension in Section 3,A, below.) This example does not reflect either hemiola or sarabande technique, but rather a technique of treating every notated second beat as a downbeat. This is shown in Ex. 156, a metrically renotated version of bars

Ex. 156. Beethoven, Piano Sonata Op. 7, 2nd movement [renotated]

1-5 of Ex. 149b.[2] Note that bar 4 of the revised version is contracted to two beats from an original three beats (Ex. 157).

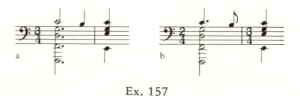

Ex. 157

B. *The Location of Large-Scale Metrical Accents*

In most pieces, the location of large-scale metrical accents can be determined by examining section divisions; but in some kinds of "through-composed" pieces, the surface texture offers no clues about large-scale divisions. The first Prelude of Bach's *Well-Tempered Clavier*, Vol. 1, is a case in point (Ex. 158). The cadences at bars 11, 19, and 32 suggest the location of some of the large-scale downbeats; but the general textural uniformity makes the metrical structure of the rest of the piece unclear.

The central analytic problem involves locating the original attack-point of the main background dominant. I regard the prolongation of the dominant chord which culminates in bar 11 as subsidiary to the dominant pedal which follows bar 19. This pedal does not commence in the literal foreground until bar 24. But since B and D are also found in bar 23, I prefer to regard the bass A♭ of that bar as an appoggiatura—with the bass G arising at a prior level at the foreground attack-point of A♭. Now let us consider the IV7 chord in bar 21. As I indicated above, in the discussion of diatonic dissonance (pp. 78-81), the progression from a I triad to a IV7 effects the seventh of the latter chord as a foreground note; bars 19-21 contain this progression, and consequently I regard the IV7 chord as a supported double-suspension chord (followed in bar 22 by a passing diminished seventh chord which tonicizes V). In the background, then, I locate V at bar 21. [3]

In view of the above considerations and in accordance with my theory of meter, bar 21 is a strong background beat, subsidiary only to the boundary time-points of the structural time-span of the piece (bars 1 and 32). Consequently, bar 21 is a stronger beat than the relatively strong middleground beats at bars 19 and 23. Nevertheless, what with the series of preceding four-bar groupings (bars 7-10, 11-14, 15-18), the well-supported

[3] In Schenker's analysis of this piece in *Fünf Urlinien-Tafeln*, Vienna, 1932, the IV chord in bar 21 is generated as a common-tone chord in the prior time-span of the initial tonic triad of the *Ursatz*. See also the English edition of this work, *Five Graphic Musical Analyses*, ed. by Felix Salzer, New York, 1969.

Ex. 158. Bach, *Well-Tempered Clavier*, Vol. 1, Prelude 1

Ex. 158 (cont.)

Ex. 158 (conclusion)

attack of E in bar 19, and the attack of the background soprano $\hat{2}$ (D) in bar 23, bars 19-22 seem to be a four-bar grouping, too—with the suspension chord (IV7) appearing to resolve (from a relatively weak beat within the grouping) at the downbeat of the next grouping (bar 23). But this is only to show that while a suspension is always *metrically* accented at the level at which it originates, other kinds of accents exist in music which may conflict with the metrical accents. Indeed, rhythmic accents frequently occur "against the beat," as indicated by dynamics and accent markings, or by the articulation of syncopated notes held through strong beats. Thus, there is no guarantee that a suspension will not be in some sense unaccented with respect to its resolution—but not *metrically* unaccented—although in general (given the choice) I would opt for an analysis in which rhythmic conflicts of this sort do not arise.

2. Foreground Configurations

A suspension may occur in all manner of foreground contexts, creating numerous interesting analytic situations. A number of these situations are described below.

A. *Delayed Suspensions*

Suspensions may be simultaneously introduced in adjacent time-spans at the same level. Given a linear sequence of three notes (Ex. 159a), the first note may be suspended into the

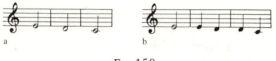

Ex. 159

time-span of the second note, at the same level at which the second note is suspended into the time-span of the third note (Ex. 159b). These are called 'sequential' suspensions. Note that the suspension of E delays the attack of the preparation D, but that neither of the suspensions itself is delayed.

The actual delay of a suspension is involved in the technique of 'overlapping' suspensions which are introduced at different levels. In Ex. 160a, the background E is suspended into the

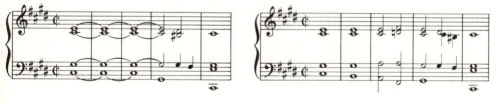

Exx. 160a and b

prior time-span (bar 4) of the soprano D♯. Subsequently, an upper neighbor, F♯, is introduced in a latter portion (bar 3) of the prior time-span of the preparation E (Ex. 160b). Then the neighbor itself is suspended into the time-span of the suspended E (Ex. 160c). As a result, the background suspension

Ex. 160c. Beethoven, Piano Sonata Op. 27/2, 1st movement [reduced]

E—which is metrically accented with respect to its resolution, D♯, at the level at which it (E) is generated as a suspension—becomes metrically unaccented with respect to that resolution, in the foreground. The background alto suspension, C♯, is also shifted to an unaccented position in bar 4 of the foreground, due to the appoggiatura, B♯, which retonicizes I after the tonicization of IV (D♮ = $\hat{6}$ in F♯ minor, the IV of C♯ minor).

Example 161c offers an alternative analysis of Ex. 160c, in which the soprano E and alto C♯ at the second quarter-note of

Ex. 161

bar 4 are regarded as linear-notes. The obvious advantage of this analysis is the description of E as a passing-note, in accordance with its weak metrical enclosure within F♯ and D♯. But the first soprano F♯ (bar 3) is now treated as an anticipation of the second F♯ (Ex. 161b), although the former F♯ is absolutely consonant and the latter is absolutely dissonant. Because of this harmonic context, I prefer to regard E in bar 4 as a delayed background suspension, rather than as a local passing-note.

In an example cited by Schenker,[4] a 6/4 suspension chord is reached at the metrically unaccented sixth bar of an eight-bar phrase (Ex. 162d). Once again the technique of overlapping

Exx. 162a, b, and c

suspensions is involved (Exx. 162b and c); but unlike the preceding example from the Moonlight Sonata, these suspensions (E and C♯, bars 5-6, Ex. 162c) overlap the *entire* prior time-span of the more background suspensions (D♯ and B♯). Subsequently (Ex. 162d), appoggiatura chords are introduced in bars 1, 3, and 5—the one in bar 5 serving to delay the 6/4 suspension chord until bar 6.

Ex. 162d. Chopin, Waltz Op. 64/2 [reduced]

The converse of the delayed suspension is the anticipated resolution, which cuts into the *latter* part of a suspension's prior time-span. G♯, the resolution of the suspended soprano A♯ in bar 1 of Ex. 163b, originally occupies the second quarter-note of that bar, as in Ex. 163a. In the course of foreground diminutions, G♯ is articulated in the prior time-span of the

4 *Der freie Satz*, pp. 184-185, and *Anhang*, Fig. 137/1, p. 97.

suspended A♯, while being totally suppressed in its original time-span. This example is taken from Schenker's *Der freie Satz*.[5]

Ex. 163. Chopin, Nocturne Op. 15/2

B. *Suspension-Extensions*

A suspension may be the preparation of a still more foreground extension of the same pitch-class into the time-span of its resolution. A suspension-extension is indicated when both the following conditions are fulfilled: 1) between the attack-point of the original suspension and that of the resolution there is at least one secondary metrical accent which is stronger than the attack-point of the resolution itself; and 2) at the secondary metrical accent, the pitch-class of the suspension is presented simultaneously with other notes which are associated with a prior attack of the resolution. In Ex. 164a, the soprano

Ex. 164. Beethoven, Piano Sonata Op. 7, Finale

suspension, G, occupies the third eighth-note, while its resolution, F, occupies the fourth eighth-note along with the corresponding linear-notes, A♭ and D. In Ex. 164b, the suspended soprano G is registrally suppressed at the third

---

[5]   Page 150, and *Anhang*, Fig. 117/1, p. 71.

eighth-note, while being extended halfway into the prior time-span of F, *qua* resolution—which is now attacked independently of its associated linear-notes, A♭ and D.

C. *Local Elaborations*

i) Arpeggiations

At the level at which a suspension is generated, the resulting linear configuration consists of a preparation, suspension, and resolution in successive adjacent time-spans. At subsequent levels, arpeggiations may be responsible for eliminating this condition of temporal adjacency.

Example 165a contains three middleground suspensions (C and D in the alto part and G in the soprano part) with durations

Ex. 165a

of a quarter-note. Due to arpeggiation, these durations are reduced to a sixteenth-note (Ex. 165b). The durations of the resolutions are likewise reduced, so that the suspensions are

Ex. 165b. Bach, Little Prelude in C

separated from their resolutions still further. But the consistent ascending direction of the arpeggiations makes for a transparent texture in which the prior linear-rhythmic relationships stand out clearly.

ii) Ornamentation

In Ex. 150b (p. 110), bar 59 comprises essentially a diminished seventh chord, three of whose notes (E, G, and B♭) are suspensions over the tonic F in the bass part. This suspension chord is arpeggiated so that during the third beat, the suspension, G, is articulated only in the third quarter of that beat. In addition, an ornamental passing-note, A, is introduced during the second beat between G and the B♭ of the arpeggiation. Note that although the passing-note A is a local displacement of G, it does not constitute its *resolution*. This is made clear through the lack of support for A in the other parts. (G resolves to F in bar 60.)

In Ex. 166, the sole foreground suspension ornament is the upper neighbor G♭ in the soprano part, bar 2. In this case,

Ex. 166. Beethoven, Piano Sonata Op. 26, 2nd movement, Trio

the foreground displacement (G♭) and the genuine resolution (E♭) occupy time-spans of equal duration. But the G♭ is unsupported, while the E♭ is attacked simultaneously with other members of the V7 chord in other parts. (The F in bar 2 is another example of a suspension-extension; see Section 2,B, above.)

Example 167, bar 1, consists of a diminished seventh suspension chord in which the soprano arpeggiation, C♭-A♭, is filled in by an accented passing note, B♭. Unlike the examples cited above, the foreground displacement (B♭) of the suspension in question (C♭) is a member of the same pitch-class as its background resolution (the tenor B♭ in bar 2). The differentiation between the two B♭'s comes from the support of the

Ex. 167. Beethoven, Piano Sonata Op. 26, 3rd movement, bars 17-20

second B♮ in the V triad, as compared to the lack of bass motion at the attack-point of the first B♮.

Like suspensions, preparations are subject to foreground ornamentation (subsequent to the levels at which the suspensions are generated). The result of such ornamentation is that it is sometimes difficult to tell precisely which notes are being suspended. Suppose that we agree that the three I6/4 chords of Ex. 168a (bars 2, 4, and 7) are double-suspension chords;

Ex. 168a. Beethoven, Piano Sonata Op. 2/1, 2nd movement, bars 1-8

where, then, are their preparations? There is no problem as far as bar 7 is concerned, since there is really just one suitable preparation chord, found back at the beginning of bar 5 (see Ex. 168b). The suspension chords of bars 2 and 4, however, are immediately preceded in the foreground by notes of the same pitch. Thus, F and A are present at the last eighth-note of bar 1, and again at the last eighth-note of bar 3. As my analysis in Ex.

Ex. 168b

168b shows, I disregard these offbeat notes as preparations, and look instead to the background tonic triad which commences at the first beat of bar 1 as the preparation of *both* suspension chords (in bars 2 and 4). In other words, I regard these suspensions as large-scale, as opposed to small-scale, extensions from preceding time-spans. The criteria in this case are fairly obvious: in bar 1 there is just one basic harmony (I), and somewhat the same is true of bar 3; and since the support for F and A is stronger in bar 1 than in bar 3, I regard the initial I triad as three bars in length at the prior level at which the V chord of bar 4 is generated. I am also influenced by the return of the soprano A in bar 4, in the same register as in its earlier appearance in bar 1. (For a contrasting analysis of this passage, cf. Ex. 442, in Felix Salzer's *Structural Hearing*.[6] Since the 16/4 chords of bars 2 and 4 are missing from this middleground sketch, I presume that Salzer regards them as foreground suspension chords prepared respectively by the chords immediately preceding them in bars 1 and 3.)

The soprano C of bar 10, Ex. 169, is a suspension that is prepared in the preceding bar. But which is actually the

Ex. 169. Haydn, *St. Antoni Chorale*

[6] Vol. 2, pp. 200-201.

preparation in bar 9, the soprano C at the beginning of the bar, or the inner-part C at the fourth eighth-note? Schenker apparently regarded the C in bar 10 as a small-scale transferred suspension, since he did not include it in his analytic sketch of this example.[7] I prefer to think of it as suspended from the earlier soprano C, prior to the generation of B♭ and A in bar 9, mainly because of its registral equivalence to that C.

D. *Suppressions*

i) Registral suppression

I have already had occasion to point out (p. 99 above) that a suspension may occur in a different octave from its preparation. This effect can be found in Ex. 123 (p. 91), where the alto B♮ of bar 1 is suspended an octave higher in the soprano part, bar 2. In Ex. 164b (p. 126), the soprano G is suspended in the tenor part at the second beat, but is returned to its higher register as a suspension-extension half a beat later. Similarly, the suspended soprano C♭ in Ex. 167, bar 1, is resolved down an octave in bar 2; but the preparation of C♭ (not shown) occurs sixteen bars earlier in the same register as the resolution (the tenor B♭ of Ex. 167, bar 2). One might be tempted to describe the suspensions in these examples as 'octave transfers'; but I think of linear connections as basically a pitch-class relationship rather than a pitch relationship and find in many cases that it is impossible to determine which of two registers is the principal one.

As a final example, Ex. 170 illustrates the registral suppression of the resolution of the suspended B in bar 2. The pitch-class of the resolution, A, is represented exclusively in the bass notes of the piano part.

---

[7] *Der freie Satz, Anhang*, Fig. 42/2, p. 16.

Ex. 170. Schumann, *Liederkreis* Op. 39, "Waldesgespräch"
[original published version]

ii) Pitch-class suppression

Total pitch-class suppression occurs much more rarely than registral suppression. The total suppression of a preparation is discussed on pp. 99-100, above (see Ex. 137). Example 171

Ex. 171. Beethoven, Piano Sonata Op. 27/2, 2nd movement

illustrates the total suppression of a resolution—in two places, bars 10 and 14. This happens in an eight-bar phrase (bars 9-16) containing numerous suspensions as a varied repetition of the preceding phrase, bars 1-8. Specifically, each soprano note which is attacked at a third beat in the first phrase is suspended into the following downbeat in the second phrase, while each soprano note which is originally attacked at a first beat is shifted to the second beat. In addition, contrast between the phrases is provided by means of octave doublings of the top part in bars 8-9 and 12-13. In the first phrase, all the notes of the top part (with the exception of A♭ in bar 4) are succeeded by linear displacements in the same register; but in two cases, the linear displacements (A♮ in bar 2 and the D♮ in bar 6) are not themselves in the top part. In the variation phrase these two displacements are left out altogether, resulting in a consistent set of second beats in which only one pitch-class is attacked. The strong resemblance of the variation phrase to the model implies the presence of the A♮ and D♮ in bars 10 and 14, in spite of their literal suppression.

iii) The implied suspension

The initial soprano motive—G♭-F-G♭—of the Trio of Beethoven's Sonata Op. 7, 3rd movement (Ex. 104, p. 80) is exploited in a remarkable way in the coda of that section (Ex. 172). In the middleground, the soprano lower neighbor-note, F,

Ex. 172. Beethoven, Piano Sonata Op. 7, 3rd movement, Trio (coda)

is present throughout bars 2 and 3 supported by four inner-part neighbor-notes—C♭, D♮, F, and A♭ (Ex. 173); but in the

Ex. 173

foreground, F is atriculated only in bar 1 as a passing-note and in bar 3 as the displacement of the appoggiatura E♭. Like the delayed F of bars 2-3, the attack of the final G♭ of the motive is forestalled in the foreground—until the second beat of bar 5; but in this case, there is no apparent predisplacement in conjunction with the delay of G♭ from its prior attack-point at beat 1 of bar 4. The non-displacement of F at this time-point is equivalent in one sense to its continued presence. Since the explicit presence of F in bar 4 would articulate it as a suspension (Ex. 174), its implied presence here makes it an 'implied suspension.'

Ex. 174

An implied suspension is an undisplaced but discontinued note which would be analyzed as an explicit suspension if its articulation continued until the attack-point of its displacement, as in Ex. 174. I do not wish to suggest, however, that every delay of a displacement constitutes an implied suspension. In Ex. 165b (p. 127), the sixteenth-note arpeggiations delay the soprano D at the third beat of bar 1, but I do not regard E, the predisplacement of D, as an implied suspension. Sixteenth-note articulations are a foreground feature of the piece from its inception, resulting in the attack of successively higher notes in a chord at later time-points within a beat. This suggests consistent delay merely due to suppression, without any sense of other notes having been substituted for them. (Ex. 165b contains explicit middleground suspension pairs in the soprano part of bar 2 [G-F] and in the alto parts of both bars [C-B and D-C]; see Ex. 165a.) In Ex. 172, bar 2, the right-hand D♮ is a resolution of the pitch-class suspension, E♭, but the left-hand delay of D♮ is due merely to foreground arpeggiations, as in Ex. 165b.

In Ex. 126, (p. 93), the attack of the bass note, F, at the second beat of bar 1 suggests that the remaining notes of the bar—F, A, and D—are delayed from that beat. Are the predisplacements, E, G, and C, suspensions at the second beat? C, in the voice part, is articulated at the second beat, but is consonant compared to D with respect to the bass F. E and G are absolutely dissonant with respect to F—like the implied suspension, F, in bar 4 of Ex. 172—but offbeat note-attacks occur consistently in almost every bar of this passage—suggesting delay merely by virtue of suppression, as in Ex. 165b and the left-hand part of Ex. 172. However, in Ex. 126, bars 3-4 are modeled after bars 1-2 in so many respects that I regard the explicit suspension of E over F in bar 3 (accompanied by the implied suspension, G, in the viola part) as sufficient justification for regarding E (and G) as implied suspensions in bar 1. Note the similar implied suspensions in bars 7 and 16. (See Ex. 83, p. 64, for a reduced score of bars 1-20.)

3. Differentiations Between Suspensions and Other Note Types

A. *The "Unprepared" Suspension Versus the Appoggiatura*

   i) The registrally unprepared suspension

The two members of a linear-pair may occur in one register —as literal pitch adjacencies—or in two or more different registers. In Ex. 175a, the soprano C♯ of bar 2 appears to be an

Ex. 175a

incomplete neighbor to the soprano D in bar 3; but the neighbor motion is incomplete only in the sense that the pitch-class D is represented in bar 1 in the bass register alone. In Ex. 175b, the pitch-class D of bar 1 is suspended into the time-span of

C♯, in the soprano register of C♯. At this level, the soprano pitch D appears to be merely an accented upper neighbor to C♯. In Ex. 175c, the passing-note E is generated between F♯

Ex. 175b   Ex. 175c. Beethoven
Piano Sonata Op. 10/3,
3rd movement

and D, creating the misleading impression that the suspended soprano D of bar 2 is an accented passing-note between E and C♯ .

For other examples of "false" appoggiaturas (registrally unprepared suspensions), see the discussions of registral suppression, pp. 99 and 131, above.

ii) Foreground interpolations between preparation and suspension

By definition, every suspension is prepared at the level at which it originates; but at a subsequent level the preparation may be suppressed in the latter part of its prior time-span. Under these conditions, the articulation of the suspension may resemble a note generated in the first place as an accented linear-note (appoggiatura). The problem is to differentiate between the, as it were, "unprepared" suspension and the genuine appoggiatura.

In Ex. 126 (p. 93), the soprano C of bar 1 is suspended at the first beat of bar 2. As a consequence of the foreground neighbor, D, in bar 1, the suspended C in bar 2 appears to be an accented linear-note. The suspended soprano F of bar 3, Ex. 132 (p. 97), appears in a similar context.

A particularly striking example of a pseudo appoggiatura is found in Ex. 149b (p. 110). Examining the reduction given in Ex. 176, we find that the tonic C of bar 1 is suspended in bar 4,

Ex. 176. Middleground sketch, Beethoven, Piano Sonata Op. 7, 2nd movement, bars 1-5

resolving to B in the same bar. But in the immediate foreground (Ex. 149b, bar 4), C is articulated as an incomplete upper neighbor to B; while at the next prior level, the arpeggiation D-A is omitted at beat 1, and C instead appears as an accented passing-note between D and B. Unlike the cases described in the preceding paragraph—in which the preparation is displaced by a foreground upper neighbor—the middle C in this passage is not linearly related to the D in bars 3-4 at any level (except as its displacement in bar 5). D is originally generated in the second and third beats of bar 4, as a passing-note between E and C, supported in the V4/2 chord; subsequently it is anticipated three beats back into bar 3 in the soprano part and articulated in its original time-span only in the tenor part. At the same time, the initial background alto C of bars 1-4 is suppressed during the three beats in which D is articulated as an anticipation. Then, the attack of D in the tenor part of bar 4 coincides with the reattack of C, *qua* background suspension. Thus, the suspended C appears to be an appoggiatura due to the combination of the suppression of C with the articulation of the anticipated D in bar 3, followed by the suppression of D (in the soprano register) with the reattack of C in bar 4.[8] (Note-suppressions are indicated in Ex. 176 by their enclosure within parentheses.)

---

[8] The metrical structure of Exx. 149 and 176 is discussed on p. 118, above.

It is always worth examining the large context in which an apparent appoggiatura occurs before ruling it out as a background suspension. Then, if the given note is not a member of the tonic triad and has not previously appeared in the piece, it is reasonable to call it an appoggiatura. In Ex. 134 (p. 98), the non-tonic soprano C♯ of bar 3 is an appoggiatura (anticipated at the last sixteenth-note of bar 2), but the rhythmically similar tonic triad member G♯ of bar 2 is a suspension.

Membership in the tonic triad does not always indicate a suspension, however. Consider Ex. 177, where the first articu-

Ex. 177. Chopin, Nocturne Op. 62/1

lation of the B major tonic triad does not occur until bar 4. The B of bar 3 arises as an accented passing-note between two members of the undisplaced V7 chord of bar 2, rather than as an "unprepared" suspension. On the other hand, in the same example, the soprano B of beat 3, bar 4, is a suspension, even though it appears in an identical four-note linear configuration and in the same harmonic context (V7). The difference between the two contexts is that in bar 3 B is articulated only in the middle of the time-span of the V7 chord, whereas in bar 4 it is first prepared in the I chord.

I am not prepared to state all the conditions for distinguishing between genuine appoggiaturas and "unprepared" suspensions. It would appear that the foreground displacement of the note in question must be given sufficient support to articulate it as a background displacement of the potential preparation; and it helps if the given note is articulated in some preceding time-span, even if not in the same register. But these are not rigid guideposts, since a genuine appoggiatura can be displaced by a well-supported note—in Ex. 178, D is a member of the V triad and E♭ is a member of the I triad, but E♭ is not

Ex. 178. Mozart, *Marriage of Figaro*, Act I, "Non so più"

a suspension all the same—and the preparation of a suspension can be suppressed in its entire prior time-span (e.g., the head-note G in Ex. 137, p. 100).

B. *The Suspension Preparation Versus the Anticipation*

Examples 179-180 illustrate the general differences between the preparation and the anticipation. In Ex. 179, the first soprano D is consonant compared to the second D. In Ex. 180, the initial soprano C is dissonant compared to the second C.

Ex. 179   Ex. 180

Since consonance and dissonance are criteria of support, we may infer that the difference between a preparation and an anticipation is that the latter receives weaker support than the note of the same pitch-class which succeeds it. Since there are numerous criteria of support, however, there is no guarantee that an anticipation is invariably dissonant compared to its successor (or, for that matter, that a preparation is invariably consonant compared to its suspension). Thus, in Ex. 181, the first soprano F is literally equal to the second F with respect to consonance, but the brevity and weak metrical position of the first F, along with the presence of the undisplaced tenor E♭,

Ex. 181. Mozart, *Marriage of Figaro*, Act IV, Finale

articulate it as an anticipation. By the same token, brevity and metrical weakness are not sufficient criteria of anticipations, as is shown by the pair of G♯'s in the voice part of Ex. 134 (p. 98), bars 1-2. In this case, consonance is again the determining factor: since the first G♯ is more consonant than the second one, the former is regarded as a preparation, not an anticipation (in spite of its brevity). In bars 2-3 of the same example, the initial C♯ is an anticipation—a view supported both by its relative brevity and dissonance.

An interesting problem arises in connection with middle-ground bass notes which are prepared in preceding adjacent time-spans, and which might therefore be analyzed as suspensions. The distinction between a bass suspension as opposed to a common-tone which supports an upper-part anticipation rests upon the relative metrical strength of the notes involved. Where metrical relationships are unambiguous, it is generally easy to make this distinction; and this is typically the case in the foreground. Thus, at the second beat of Ex. 182, the soprano D is

Ex. 182   Ex. 183

regarded as an anticipation, and the bass C is not regarded as a suspension, because C (at the second beat) is metrically unaccented with respect to its displacement, B. On the other hand, in Ex. 183, C is regarded as a suspension at the third beat, because (among other reasons) it is metrically accented with respect to B. In the middleground, however, where time-spans are subject to the alteration operations, metrical relationships often elude easy detection. For example, in bars 5-9 of Ex. 184a,[9] where there are two configurations involving rhythmic

Ex. 184a. Bach *Well-Tempered Clavier,* Vol. 1, Predule 1 [reduced]

shifting at a middleground level, the analytic options are to regard the soprano D in bar 6 and C in bar 8 as anticipations (Ex. 184b), or the bass C in bar 6 and B in bar 8 as suspensions

Ex. 184b

(Ex. 184c). The choice depends upon metrical criteria; but there is no obvious metrical pattern in Ex. 184a upon which to base the choice. In this case, a solution is found in the sequen-

Ex. 184c

---

[9] Example 184a represents a reduced version of bars 1-11, Ex. 158, p. 120, above.

tial soprano groupings, A-D in bars 5-6 and G-C in bars 7-8. Since I would generally consider the higher note of a note-pair as metrically accented with respect to the lower note (other things being equal), I regard the higher notes (A and G) as metrically accented with respect to the lower notes (D and C). Consequently, I analyze the soprano notes in bars 6 and 8 as metrically weak anticipations, and the bass notes in the same bars as common-tones rather than suspensions (as in Ex. 184b).

Bar 2 of Ex. 184a presents another choice between a bass suspension (C) and upper-part anticipations (D and F). I regard the upper notes as anticipations for the following reasons: 1) anticipations are found at a middleground level, as described in the preceding paragraph, suggesting that the anticipation operation is a general feature of the piece; 2) the very groupings which lend support to the analysis of the anticipations in bars 6 and 8 suggest regular two-bar groupings as a feature at various levels of the piece; and since the two-bar groupings start at odd-numbered bars, bar 3 is preferred over bar 2 as the time-point at which D and F originate: and 3) at the very end of the piece (bar 33, Ex. 158, p. 122) an unambiguously metrically unaccented D is presented as an anticipation in a four-bar passage which is very similar to bars 1-4—supporting the notion that anticipations, and anticipated D's in particular, are characteristic of the piece.

C. *The Suspension Versus the Common-Tone*

Once a note has been generated in a given time-span, it can be subsequently divided into two or more attacks within that time-span—this is the case in Ex. 185b, where the second C is

Ex. 185

known as a 'common-tone.' Observe that the second C *looks* like an extension of the first C; in reality it is not an extension, because it is present—as an unattacked pitch-class—in the same time-span at the prior level (Ex. 185a). By contrast, a suspension *is* an extension of a given note beyond its prior time-span. The resemblance between a common-tone and a suspension makes it essential to consider the total context in which a given note appears as a potential extension, in order to evaluate which kind of note it is.

If a predisplacement is accented with respect to its displacement at just one metrical level (Ex. 186a), the suspension of the

Ex. 186

predisplacement will make it accented at two metrical levels with respect to its displacement (Ex. 186b). But a predisplacement can be accented at two metrical levels with respect to its displacement to begin with (Ex. 187). So, at a secondary

Ex. 187

metrical accent (i.e., a beat which is strong at one metrical level but weak at a higher one, like the third beat of a 4/4 bar) a predisplacement may be either a suspension (Ex. 186b) or a common-tone (Ex. 187). The analytic choice between a suspension and a common-tone in such a case is usually determined by harmonic criteria.

i) Dissonant contexts

A predisplacement which has a secondary metrical accent is normally a suspension at that time-point if it is more dissonant at that time-point than at its primary metrical accent. Taken by itself, the soprano line of Ex. 188 suggests that in bar 2, F♯

Ex. 188. Mozart, *Ave Verum* K. 618

might be regarded as a common-tone and G as an anticipation of the longer held G in bar 3. But the harmonic context in bars 1-2 articulates F♯ as a suspension (see Ex. 189); and therefore,

Ex. 189

the quarter-note G is more appropriately analyzed as the resolution of the suspended F♯, than merely as an anticipation of G in bar 3. (The consequence of analyzing the G of bar 2 as an anticipation is shown in the reduction given in Ex. 190. The

Ex. 190

problem here is that there is no contextual justification for the generation of the bass G in bar 2.)

On the other hand, if a predisplacement is absolutely dissonant at its primary metrical accent to begin with, and remains so at its secondary metrical accent, then the predisplacement is simply a dissonant common-tone at the secondary metrical accent. In Ex. 191, B♯ is absolutely dissonant at the second

Ex. 191. Beethoven, Piano Sonata Op. 78, Finale

beat of bar 1. B♯ is supported in exactly the same harmonic context at the first beat as well, and therefore is a common-tone at beat 2, which is to say that it is generated throughout its entire foreground time-span at one and the same level, as a dissonant accented lower neighbor.

I should add that it would be pointless to generate a diatonic dissonator at a secondary metrical accent of a given note (in order to facilitate the displacement of the given note in its original time-span) since the resulting harmonic context would imply an analysis of the given note as a suspension, rather than a common-tone, at the secondary accent. Even if Ex. 192 is meant to be a derivation from Ex. 193, it reduces nonetheless directly to Ex. 194. (See the discussion of diatonic dissonance, pp. 78ff., above.)

Ex. 192   Ex. 193   Ex. 194

In exceptional circumstances, relative dissonance at a secondary metrical accent does *not* indicate a suspension. The tenor E♭ at beat 2 of bar 2, Ex. 195, is not a suspension, in spite of

Ex. 195. Bach, Cantata No. 159, Chorale: "Jesu, deine Passion"

its conversion from an absolute consonance at beat 1 to an absolute dissonance at beat 2. In the middleground, its displacement D♭ is introduced at the third beat, along with the bass note G. Then F is introduced in the bass as a foreground passing-note between E♭ and G, while D♭ is anticipated at the fourth eighth-note.

The same kind of analytical problems which arise in distinguishing common-tones from suspensions also arise when one tries to distinguish suspension-"continuations" from suspension-extensions (see p. 126, above). In Ex. 196b, the suspended G of

Ex. 196

Ex. 196a is divided into two attacks. The second attack represents a continuation of the suspension, the equivalent of a common-tone. On the other hand, the soprano G at the fourth eighth-note of Ex. 164b (p. 126) is a suspension-extension, due to the relative dissonance of the reference-interval, G-A♭, as compared to the reference interval, G-B♭ at the third eighth-note.

ii) Consonant contexts

I have already discussed the conditions under which consonant suspensions arise (pp. 84-86, above). The analytic choice between a consonant suspension and a consonant common-tone is determined by the rhythmic pattern of associated notes in other parts. In Ex. 109 (p. 84), the final soprano E♭ is associated with other members of the I6 chord, while the preceding passing-note D is associated with the supporting linear-notes, A♭ and F. Therefore, in the last bar, D is either a suspension, or else it is a common-tone and G and B♭ are initially anticipations. Since a common-tone is generated at the same level as its "preparation", the analysis of D as common-tone necessarily entails generating D in a total time-span which is syncopated (assuming the accuracy of the bar lines, as I do in this case). It is clearly preferable to regard the E♭, a background member of the tonic triad, as having originated—with the other members of the I6 triad—at the first beat of the bar.

At beat 2, bar 3, Ex. 168a (p. 129), the soprano C is a consonant suspension[10] despite the dissonance of its displacement, B♮, because of the association of B♮ with the bass neighbor-note E♮ that occurs at the second beat. I prefer to think of E as originating at the second beat, rather than half a beat later—particularly since in the motivically similar third beat, F and A clearly originate at the beginning of that beat. Similarly, in bars 9-10 of Ex. 197a, the soprano G is a suspension despite the relative consonance of D-G compared to D-A♭, because of the prior rhythmic association of D and A♭ (see Exx. 197b and c).

---

[10] Strictly speaking, a consonant suspension is a note which is more consonant as suspension than as preparation. However, a suspension may also be considered consonant if it is more consonant than it resolution. In bar 3, Ex. 168a, the soprano C is more dissonant as a suspension at beat 2 than as its preparation in beat 1 (with reference to the bass part), but is consonant compared to its resolution, B♮, in beat 2.

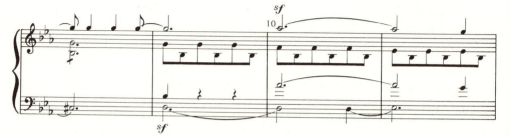

Ex. 197. Beethoven, Symphony No. 3, 1st movement

A contrasting illustration is found in Ex. 198a. At the second beat of bar 1, the soprano D is metrically accented and

Ex. 198a

consonant with respect to its displacement C. But all the linear-notes associated with C are attacked simultaneously with it at the fourth eighth-note, and D gets the same harmonic support at beat 2 as at beat 1. Therefore, D is analyzed as an accented common-tone at beat 2. The example represents an analysis of Ex. 198b.

Ex. 198b. Beethoven, Piano Sonata Op. 7, Finale

This brings to a close my study of suspensions. While not pretending that the study is exhaustive—I note in particular the absence of any show of dealing with suspensions in a historical perspective—I hope that it is reasonably comprehensive. The reader is cordially invited to communicate any responses that he may have to my theories of meter and suspensions, by writing to me in care of the publisher.

APPENDIX

METRICAL RELATIONS AT BACKGROUND
AND MIDDLEGROUND LEVELS

In Chapter Three, I have formulated a theory of meter
pertinent to all structural levels of a tonal piece. The analytic
implications of this theory are that the bars, phrases, and
sections of a piece are metrically related to one another like
beats within a single bar. In order to demonstrate bar-groupings
at relatively background levels, I offer here a metrical analysis
of the slow movement of Beethoven's Piano Sonata Op. 13 (Ex.
199). As I indicated in the discussion of the opening phrase of
the slow movement of Beethoven's Piano Sonata Op. 7 (p. 118,
above), one cannot always accept at face value the notation of
local beat relationships; in the case at hand, however, each
notated downbeat is in fact the strongest beat within its bar.
Therefore, I have ignored the foreground metrical relationships
within each bar and have derived metrical values only as far
down into the middleground as necessary for the generation of
all the bar-lines of the piece (see Ex. 200).

We are all quite accustomed to finding bars of equal size
throughout long stretches of tonal music, which raises the possibility of discovering metrical units of equal size at higher levels
as well. The consistent duple organization within each bar of
Ex. 199 certainly suggests the possibility of two-bar groupings
at higher levels. For a start, bars 1-2 form a reasonable grouping,
inasmuch as the I6 chord in bar 2 bisects the time-span enclosed
by the two I5/3 chords in bars 1 and 3. But a problem arises in
connection with the next set of two bars, since the dominant
cadence in bar 4 metrically outweighs the pitch events in bars 3
and 5. If we now proceed with bar 4 as a strong beat, then the
rest of the refrain[1] to bar 16 can be analyzed in two-bar pairs,

---

[1] The movement is in rondo form, consisting of five sections and a coda:
1) refrain, bars 1-16; 2) first episode, bars 17-29; 3) refrain, bars 29-36; 4)
second episode, bars 37-51; 5) refrain, bars 51-66; and 6) coda, bars 67ff.

Ex. 199. Beethoven, Piano Sonata Op. 13, 2nd movement

Ex. 199 (cont.)

Ex. 199 (conclusion)

starting at each even-numbered bar. Moreover, since the metrically weak bar 9 is a varied repetition of bar 1, bar 1 can be thought of as a weak intervening beat between a suppressed bar 0 and bar 2. In this light, bars 1-2 represent a syncopated time-span, since the attack-point of bar 2 is a stronger beat than that of either bar 1 or bar 3 (see Ex. 69, p. 58 and Ex. 200, levels 7-8).

(The concept of bar 0 arises in connection with a piece starting on an upbeat. An initial zero-numbered bar is most typically found in a piece in which the first complete bar is preceded by one or more unaccompanied melodic notes [see Ex. 131d, p. 96]. However, the notion of bar 0 need not be limited to pieces beginning with incomplete bars; it is applicable to any piece commencing at a relatively weak beat. The upbeat effect is substantially diminished in cases where the initial upbeat is itself a complete bar [as in Ex. 199], insofar as the first beat is stronger than the other beats *within* that bar. In classical music, the usual justification for regarding the first whole bar as an upbeat is that all the initial metrical strongpoints [cadences] occur at even-numbered bars [again, as in Ex. 199]. It should be noted that in the background, the structural time-span invariably starts on a strong beat [see Chapter Three, Sections 1-3]; this beat is called "bar 1" unless it is suppressed in the foreground, in which case it numerically precedes bar 1, as bar 0, or possibly even as a minus-numbered bar.)

Looking at the opening sixteen-bar time-span of Ex. 199 (starting with the suppressed bar 0 and ending with the cadence at the beginning of bar 16), we find four 4-bar and also two 8-bar groupings—supporting the notion that bisection is a metrical feature of all levels of the piece. But we have only to look ahead to the first episode to find phrases of seven and six bars, respectively. And other sections of the piece are also characterized by irregularly sized phrases. In this respect, the piece is not at all atypical of the tonal literature; i.e., we cannot expect to find pieces breaking down into ever-larger sections with bar numberings fitting neatly into the series of powers of 2. In this respect I am in complete agreement with Edward T. Cone, when

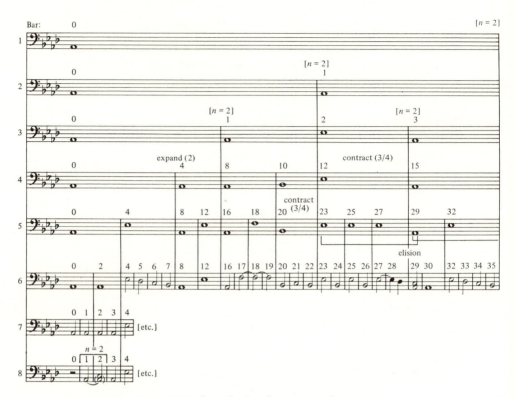

Ex. 200 Metrical analysis of Ex. 199 (bars 1-35)

he writes of "the shortcoming of all attempts to invoke mechanically at higher levels the metrical arrangement of beats within a measure (or of measures within a hypermeasure)."[2]

All the same, just as foreground meter is by nature uniform, I am not prepared to think differently of meter at higher levels. Rather, I think that background and middleground time-spans are initially of uniform size, but are typically subjected to the alteration operations (see pp. 62-67, above), which effect subsequent time-spans of irregular size. In the present case, we can infer a background bisection of the structural time-span, as indicated in the foreground by the virtual subdivision of the movement into two halves, each with its own continuous rhythmic figuration—sixteenth-notes in the first half (to bar

[2] *Musical Form and Musical Performance*, New York, 1968, p. 40.

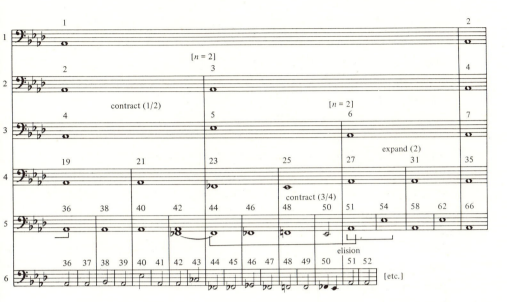

Ex. 200 Metrical analysis of Ex. 199 (bars 36-66)

36), and triplet sixteenth-notes thereafter. These two parts are not precisely identical in foreground size, however, and it would be a mistake to ignore the difference. The first part consists of 36 bars, whereas the second part consists of just 30 bars (not counting the coda, which I deal with separately below). The 6:5 ratio (i.e., 36:30 divided by 6) of these sizes raises the possibility of subdividing the structural time-span into eleven parts, as an alternative to exact bisection; but there is nothing in the organization of the movement to support this approach. Indeed, the sixteenth-note half of the movement consists of five—not six—phrases, and the triplet sixteenth-note half consists of just four phases, implying at most a possible subdivision into nine parts (5:4), rather than eleven. But there is also reason to reject 9 as a background divisor—namely the fact that the principal non-tonic cadence of the second half of the movement (located at bar 44) falls considerably less than halfway into that part. Now if this half consisted of four parts in the background (as it does in the foreground), then its second strongest beat would be at the beginning of the third of those parts (bar 51); but the strength of the F♭ major cadence (notated as E major) in bar 44 outweighs bar 51 as a metrical accent. The solution is to regard bar 44 as the original midpoint of the second half of the movement, with subsequent alteration operations accounting for the foreground discrepancies in the sizes of the time-spans on either side of that midpoint. In the background, then, the second half of the movement consists itself of just two halves.

In accordance with my view that background pitch structures are relatively simple compared to the complex pitch structures of the foreground (see pp. 17-19, above), I am prejudiced in favor of simple metrical relationships at background levels. That is, given the choice between a lower or higher n, I would generally prefer the lower. (You will note that I have chosen $n = 2$ at levels 1 and 2 of Ex. 200.) But I would also feel obliged to justify any subsequent alterations effecting irregularly sized phrases and sections in the foreground. I shall therefore comment on the various alteration operations introduced at levels 3-5 of Ex. 200.

(Before proceeding, a word is in order regarding the construction of Ex. 200. Each individual staff signifies a structural level, beginning with level 1 in the background. The bar numbers change from level to level, according to the divisors introduced in conjunction with the various operations applied at any one level. Thus, there are just two full bars at level 1, as a consequence of $n = 2$. Subsequent divisions result in a total of four full bars at level 2; therefore, bar 1 at level 1 is renumbered as bar 2 at level 2, and similarly bar 2 at level 1 becomes bar 4 at level 2. Observe that the operations applied at level 3 produce just seven full bars. This follows from the fact that bars 1, 2, and 4 of level 2 are bisected at level 3, while bar 3 of level 2 is contracted to one-half its prior size, equaling one full bar at level 3. The bar numbering becomes considerably more complex at levels 4 and 5, but the procedures are the same. It should aid the reader to know that the bar numbers at level 5 coincide with those of the actual piece.)

I regard the varied reprises in bars 9-16 and 59-66 of Ex. 199 as relatively foreground expansions of the preceding eight-bar phrases.[3] Thus, in the middleground, I think of each instance of the refrain (represented at level 3 of Ex. 200 by bars 0, 3, and 6) as equivalent to an eight-bar section in the foreground. The expansions of the first and third instances of the refrain are introduced at level 4.

In order to explain the contraction of bar 2 at level 2 into bar 4 at level 3, I remind the reader that there are two beats at level 1 and four beats at level 2. The two new beats at level 2 (bars 1 and 3) are represented in the foreground by the two main non-tonic cadences of the movement, at bars 23 and 44. Observe that the first of these non-tonic cadences, at bar 23, is preceded by the initial sixteen-bar refrain and the first phrase of episode 1, and is followed by the second phrase of that episode and then the refrain again. The F♭ cadence in bar 44 is likewise *followed* by a phrase of episode 2 and the refrain, but is preceded (in part 2, which commences with the triplet sixteenth-notes after bar 36) by one phrase of episode 2 alone—i.e., without the combination of refrain and a phrase of episode which occurs before the E♭ cadence at bar 23 in part 1. Of course, the second episode is preceded by the refrain which brings part 1 to an end, but I do not regard that refrain as belonging pivotally to both halves of the movement because of the association of its sixteenth-note figuration with part 1. I am more willing to believe that the first phrase of episode 2 itself represents a disguised version of the refrain, since it contains certain elements of the refrain transposed into the key of F♭ major. Starting in bar 41, we find that the main soprano note, A♭, is followed in bar 42 by G♭ (F♯) and C♭ (B♮), with the latter two notes as members of a V4/2-I6 progression, corresponding to the identical melodic-harmonic progression in bars 1-2 of the refrain.

---

[3] Since bars 51-58 themselves constitute a variation of bars 1-8, bars 59-66 can be most accurately described as the varied reprise of a variation.

Moreover, the succession of two ascending melodic fourths in bars 1-3 of the refrain (Bb-Eb and Eb-Ab) is represented in bars 42-43 by three accented melody notes, F♯-B-E; while the final melody notes of bars 43-44 (B-D♯-E) are a transposition of the Eb-G-Ab which melodically outline the background V-I progression of bars 4-8 of the refrain. In view of these correspondences, I believe it is reasonable to think of the first phrase of the second episode as a contraction representing refrain and episode alike.

Level 4 introduces another contraction, this time in part 1. The Eb cadence at bar 23 bisects part 1 at level 3, and further bisections are introduced at level 3, corresponding to bars 16 and 29 in the foreground. Examination of the foreground reveals that bar 3 at level 3 (bar 29 in the foreground) falls less than halfway between bars 2 and 4 (bars 23 and 36, respectively). In other words, the refrain which commences at bar 29 is seven bars long, but the larger grouping to which it belongs is only thirteen, not fourteen, bars long. Another peculiarity of this passage is that unlike the beginning of the varied reprise in bar 9, which *follows* the cadence in bar 8, the beginning of the refrain in bar 29 is itself a cadential ending (of the preceding episode). The idea of generating the refrain in the final seven bars of a thirteen-bar time-span cannot be countenanced, since these seven bars represent a syncopated portion of that time-span; and in any case, the refrain is basically eight bars long, corresponding to the length of the initial refrain and its reprise (bars 0-8 and 8-16). So I regard both the second part of the first episode and the following refrain as initially equivalent to eight bars in length. The second part of the episode is subsequently reduced to six bars and is followed by an elision at bar 29 (see p. 66, above), accounting for the missing bar at the beginning of the ensuing refrain.

Just as there is a 4:3 ratio between the time-spans of parts 1 and 2 at level 3, there is a similar ratio between the first and second subsections of the first episode—i.e., between bars 8-12 and 12-15—at level 4. At level 5, two other contractions are introduced. One occurs in the first phrase of the first episode (bars 20-23), where the time-span of V/V, B♭, is shortened from four to three bars, producing still another 4:3 ratio (between bars 16-20 and 20-23); the other occurs in the second phrase of the second episode (bars 48-51), again with a resulting 4:3 ratio (between bars 44-48 and 48-51). In light of the expansions represented by the varied reprises of the refrain at the beginning and ending of the movement, there is a certain symmetrical aspect to the metrical relations of the piece: in addition to the expansions of the *first* and *last* refrains, the *first* half of the *first* episode (bars 16-23) and the *second* half of the *second* episode (bars 44-51) are contracted to seven-eighths their prior (equal-sized) time-spans. Another correspondence (in this case, non--symmetrical) is the elision which occurs at the end of each episode, as the refrain recommences (in bars 29 and 51).

The coda (which lies outside the structural time-span of the movement, see p. 51, above) is essentially a seven-bar time-span which appropriately reflects the prevailing 4:3 ratios of the movement proper. In the first four bars (starting at bar 66), there is a harmonic rhythm of one chord to a bar, while in the next three bars the tempo of harmonic change is twice as fast. Also, the further extension of the coda by half a bar (from beat 1 of bar 73 to the fermata at the second beat of that bar) produces a diminution of the 4:3 ratio in the second part of the coda: two bars in higher registers (bars 70-71) are followed by one and a half bars in lower registers.

INDEX OF DEFINITIONS AND EXPLICATIONS

165